GW00535655

GREENISLAND PRESS

CAPTIVE COLUMNS

An Underground Prison Press
1865–2000

EOGHAN MAC CORMAIC

CAPTIVE COLUMNS

An Underground Prison Press
1865–2000

Greenisland Press

This edition published in 2024
Greenisland Press, Belfast
e-mail: info@greenislandpress.ie

An imprint of Elsinor Verlag (Elsinor Press), Coesfeld, Germany
e-mail: info@elsinor.de
website: www.elsinor.de

© Eoghan Mac Cormaic 2024
All rights reserved
Author contact: eoghanmaccormaic@gmail.com

Cover design: Seán Mistéil and Eoghan Mac Cormaic
Printed in Germany

ISBN: 978-3-949573-05-7

ALSO BY EOGHAN MAC CORMAIC

Pluid (Coiscéim 2021)

On the Blanket (An Fhuiseog 2022)

Macallaí Cillín (Coiscéim 2023)

the pen behind the wire (Greenisland Press 2023)

Gaeil agus Géibheann (Coiscéim 2024)

Tá an t-údar thar a bheith buíoch as cúnamh airgid Chumann na Méirleach Poblachtach Éireannach, Béal Feirste, (the Irish Republican Felons Association, Belfast) mar phátrún foilsitheoireacht an tsaothair, *Captive Columns*.

The author gratefully acknowledges the financial assistance of Cumann Na Méirleach Poblachtach Éireannach (the Irish Republican Felons Association, Belfast) as a patron towards the publication of *Captive Columns*.

DEDICATED TO THE MEMORY OF

Brian Campbell (1960–2005)

A friend, comrade and a great writer. A man of imagination
Editor of *Scairt Amach*, *The Captive Voice* and *An Phoblacht*

CONTENTS

INTRODUCTION

While researching the use and teaching of the Irish language over a span of one hundred and thirty years among republican prisoners, from Fenian times to modern times, I would regularly come across references to prisoners producing their own newspapers and news-sheets. Sometimes these papers were created as an outlet for prison writings—poetry, prose, political analyses, et cetera—in English and in Irish, as well as being platforms for political discussion, education, humour and creativity. These publications were a part of, yet also a tangent to, the field I was investigating. But as I continued, I became convinced that as a topic these jail journals merited study in their own right.

Finding the prison newspapers—or as comprehensive a list of newspapers as possible—was going to be a challenge, since many of the papers were ephemeral by nature: single pages, single editions, whimsical productions. They were subject to the vagaries of prison life: searches, censorship, sudden transfers, releases and even, sadly, executions. That fragments and copies survived at all is incredible: a full seven-issue set of a prison-ship paper from the 1860s or a hand-written set of newspapers from a prison camp in 1921 which survive to this day are remarkable. So too are the three collections of newspapers produced in Long Kesh in the 1970s and kept safely for almost fifty years by Séanna Breathnach, Paddy McMenamin, Brendan Curran and others; or the file of prison materials from Portlaoise maintained by Anne O'Sullivan. The National Library and Kilmainham Jail[1] also hold prison papers and are to be thanked for their safe custody of these important, if overlooked artefacts.

Republican prison autobiographies provide some clues, sometimes no more than a passing reference to the name of a prison paper or journal. Occasionally the author would give details of the title and its

---

1   In most instances I have used the spelling 'Jail' in place of the more archaic 'Gaol', except within a quote or an extant reference.

content, or perhaps an anecdote as to how it was produced or distributed. The role of the *mosquito press* is to bite and move on, but frequently, however, the papers moved on too quickly and no copies remain extant.

Choosing and quoting sources also caused a personal dilemma for me at times. Some of those who had been active on the republican side pre-1921 sent former comrades to their doom in prison cells in 1922-24, while ex-republicans from the Civil War locked former comrades away in prison camps in the 1940s. Some witnesses from the 1940s and 1960s in northern jails turned on former comrades in the 1970s and later. Old prison wing-mates would shun former associates in later years. And some would simply fade away. For this research I took a decision to treat each source at face value, looking at their contributions *at the time*, being *of the time*, and left their later life-paths to themselves.

And so, Éarnán de Blaghd, the republican editor of *Glór na Carcrach* in Belfast Prison in 1918 becomes Ernest Blythe the Free State cabinet bête noir of Peadar O'Donnell's musings in *The Book of Cells* in Mountjoy Prison in 1922. In the 1930s he becomes the propagandist speech writer for Eoin O'Duffy and the fascist Blueshirts, before morphing into the Abbey Theatre director who briefly appeared to cultivate the prison writing of Brendan Behan in the 1940s. But, for the purposes of this book his various personae are treated as separate entities. His reminiscences, like those of many others from which I draw information—editors and writers of prison newspapers who, post-prison, sometimes took political positions which were at odds with the idealism and ideals which framed their earlier lives—are all important.

This study, therefore, is sometimes more about the *produce* than the producers of prison newspapers.

Sixty 'journals' are included in this book (a full list is included in the Appendix), spanning just over one hundred and thirty years of imprisonment and ranging from untitled sheets of toilet paper with coded news patiently pin-pricked in indentations by Fenian prisoners, to the glossy *Glór Gafa* of the 1990s. Some were satirical, some serious, some were written in English, some were in Irish. They varied from single sheets to thirty and forty-page journals. Some had text only, others had text with illustrations. These journals are a vital part of our understanding of what imprisonment was and how republican prisoners dealt with it, challenged it, and ultimately overcame it.

To all the scribes and those who scratched their names, mo mhíle buíochas libh.

For thousands of years, century after century, records have been lost. Some remain and some over time have been repeated and revered, some long forgotten or apocryphal. All these sources have their place in the history of the recording and dissemination of news. In some future time, perhaps not so far from now, all our news will be electronic, all our media, social. The methods of passing on news change over time and for one epoch the printed word, on paper or on some similar medium, was supreme.

Small groups, either pre-selected or self-selected, want to record their passing stories and share them with others of the group. Newsletters became a stock item in keeping members of any community bonded and informed of the group's news and activities. It is no surprise then, that a group such as a prison-wing of prisoners, identifying under a common cause, should want to record their own story too. The past one hundred and fifty years has seen many periods of imprisonment and during almost every one of them prisoners could be found producing 'newspapers': designed, written, distributed, and read in the close quarters of the various places of captivity, whether in stone buildings, barbed wire prison camps or even on boats at sea or moored out from the coast.

Restrictions, consistent with prison rules and prison life, often meant that the newspapers were transient and temporary – the material of short duration or durability. The confinement of prison has meant that the number of surviving examples is very limited. Scarce copies were sometimes smuggled out of the prisons or brought out at the end of periods of imprisonment by prisoners as souvenirs. Some newspapers were handwritten, some were copied by hand, some were read to a captive audience, and some were even sold within the prison. Some of these newspapers became prized trophies to both prison staff and prisoners. In the final years of the 1980s–1990s, one magazine, *An Glór Gafa*, went into full-scale production, written in various prisons, collated, and edited in the H-Blocks and printed and sold in Ireland and the USA.

In this study of prison journals, I have used a wide range of possible sources, including previously unpublished material, memoirs, minutes of meetings and published autobiographies in both Irish and in English. I have also searched the Bureau of Military History's written records for reminiscences of jail life from 1916-24, recorded in the wider story of the time. Included here is a comprehensive look at the many prison journals and newspapers, some without name or title produced by republican prisoners since Fenian times.

Included also is material from three previously unpublished compilations, a memoir by Belfast IRA volunteer Liam P Ó Muireadhaigh, which spanned periods of imprisonment in the nineteen twenties, thirties and forties; a set of minutes recording three years of the activities of a prison group, An Cumann Gaelach, which existed in Belfast and Derry jails in the 1930s and 1940s; and a short memoir by Eamonn Boyce recalling his prison experience in the nineteen fifties and sixties. I am grateful to have had the opportunity to give life to these old documents and, via the documents, to provide some 'glimpses' of Irish felons' lives.

I present this book as a comprehensive, but not necessarily definitive, list of publications. If there are titles which I have overlooked I would welcome any further leads towards completeness.

Cells below deck on the
convict ship *Success*

FROM FENIANS
TO FRONGOCH
1865–1917

Architect's view of the gentry taking an unruffled
Sunday stroll in the silent Pentonville wings

TO AUSTRALIA BOUND

In 1867 a young man, John Sarsfield Casey, a Fenian from Cork, was transported to Australia. He had already spent more than two years in prison; including a remand in both the City and County prisons in Cork, followed, after sentencing, by a short stay in Mountjoy Prison in Dublin. His prison path then saw him travelling through a number of prisons in Britain beginning in 1866 in Pentonville Prison. Later, Pentonville would be forever associated with the republican struggle. It was in Pentonville that Roger Casement was executed in 1916. In 1917, when a decision was taken to release unconditionally the remaining prisoners who had been sentenced in the aftermath of the Easter Rising, many of them were brought centrally to Pentonville to spend a night there before the releases took place.

But all of that was fifty years after John Casey first set foot in the prison.

Pentonville was a mere twenty-two years in operation by the time of his committal and its 520 cells spread out from a central 'circle' in four radial wings, following a design first employed by English-born architect John Haviland, the architect of the Eastern State Penitentiary in Philadelphia, built in 1834. Prisons in the USA were providing theories of imprisonment and control which European governments in Italy, France and Britain were eager to learn from. The Eastern State Penitentiary imposed a regime of 'separation' (solitary confinement) while the New York prison system employed a regime of 'strict silence'. The British penal authorities, in their benign way, decided to combine both and so the separation *and* silent system was brought into being.

Pentonville was a 'model' prison, a huge, silent tomb where all communication between prisoners was forbidden and punishable by harsh penalties. At one stage prisoners were even forced to wear a peaked cap to cover their eyes so that they would not see other human faces. This was an era where puritanical and almost fanatical doctrine led by the Quaker Jeremy Bentham, the 'reformer' Elizabeth Fry, and

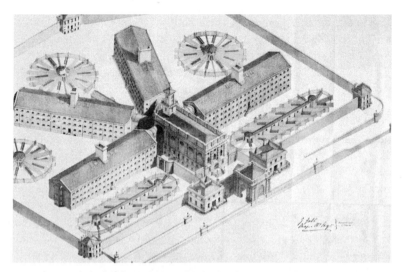

Pentonville Prison showing almost 600 single cells with individual and isolated exercise yards. (Image courtesy of Mike Egan)

others, held that prisoners must be made to repent and atone for wrongdoing and believed that 'strict silence, and a judicious plan of solitary confinement, will be found the most powerful of all moral instruments for correction of the guilty'.[2]

Bentham was also the creator of the prison 'panopticon' theory: a system which advocated a minimum number of guards strategically positioned to 'see all' (hence, *panopticon*) prisoners in such a way that the prisoners would not or could not be certain that they were being so observed at any given time. Pentonville, however, was not strictly speaking, a panopticon, but a series of smaller panopticons, as in, for example, the design of the exercise yards.

2   *The Eighth Report of the Committee of the Society for the Improvement of Prison Discipline, and for the Reformation of Juvenile Offenders* (1832) London.

Casey and his comrades successfully subverted the separation system repeatedly as they awaited news of their exile to Australia. In 1867 Casey's final stop in Britain before transportation was in the truly grim conditions of Portland Prison where O'Donovan Rossa would suffer so much. Rossa was, in fact, a prison contemporary of Casey.

It was during the young Corkman's time in the regime in Pentonville Prison that he first discovered how prisoners learned to disseminate news and communications even under the most acute penal conditions. Casey had arrived in Pentonville on 16 January 1866 having been sentenced in Cork the previous month to seven years Penal Servitude for the 'crime' of Treason Felony.[3] As he later wrote in his account of those years: 'separate confinement ... was the most severe part of a prisoner's imprisonment, consisting as it does of total seclusion for twenty-three-and-a-quarter hours out of every twenty-four hours'.[4] The three-quarter hour daily exercise period was spent in the yard and it, too, was conducted in accordance with the rule of silence and isolation.

Circular cages, or rectangles with rounded ends, like stadia, were constructed in prison yards. As the illustrations from the plans of Pentonville Prison in the 1840s show, these exercise cages were an integral part of the prison and not some later addition. In Pentonville there were: '114 separate exercise yards each yard being 43 feet long by an average breadth of about 10 feet'.[5] This number of yards 'is a proportion of more than one fourth the number of prisoners, so that, taking into account those prisoners who obtain their exercise by pumping water the remainder get an hours exercise each in about four hours in the course of the day.'[6]

The yards were a central feature of the *Separate System*—a system which would drive many prisoners to insanity. The circular cages and stadia were divided into multiple triangular segments and strips, each divided from the others by walls with a small, roofed shelter but open to the sky. The prison guards patrolled the centre, observing all the individual exercise yards which were physically separate from each other. The circumference of the cage was made of steel bars. Prisoners entered via a central passageway directly facing the gate leading from the wing. Their only journey each day was from their cell to the exercise

3   John Sarsfield Casey (2005) *The Galtee Boy.* Dublin: University College Dublin Press (P.156).

4   John Sarsfield Casey (2005) *The Galtee Boy.* Dublin: University College Dublin Press (P.158).

5   *Report of the Surveyor-General of Prison on the Construction of Pentonville Prison,* (1844) London: HMSO (P.43).

6   *Report of the Surveyor-General of Prison on the Construction of Pentonville Prison,* (1844) London: HMSO (P.31).

yard and back. Prisoners would be aware that some comrade might, or might not be walking forward and back in an adjoining segment. However, the rule of silence was strictly imposed and prisoners could not speak to ask who was there. Exercise, therefore, was in effect, alone. The rest of the time was spent working in the dimly-lit cells, picking oakum on the highly polished floors.

Oakum was the product of picking lengths (junks) of tarred rope apart to recycle the fibre to make mats or to make caulking. It was soul-destroying, tedious work and painful on the fingers, while the daily quantity was weighed at the beginning and end of the work period and any loss of oakum from the twist (where tar was not picked fully from the fibres for example) was a punishable offence. The isolation was extreme, the painful monotony of the work detested by prisoners. Recalling his time in charge of the punishment cells half a century later in 1920s Dartmoor Prison the Governor B.D. Grew wrote that: 'Even those men hardened in the prison life of those days found the task extremely difficult, and a newcomer to it would find his fingernails torn and his fingertips blistered at the end of the first day. And that of course made the task the following day even more painful'.[7] The tedium of picking oakum was immortalised in the Irish language song 'Ócum an Phríosúin',[8] where the poet Tom Neaine Choilm Ó Lochlainn bemoans his punishment in prison for póitín making:

Molaim sú an ghráin eorna go deo deo 'gus a choíche
Nach mairg nach mbíonn tóir ar Rí Seoirse ar a dhéanamh
Seán Ford a bheith ina ghiúistis, is chomhairleodh na daoine
Mar is chuir mise ag foghlaim le ócam a spíonadh
Is randa dideloram 'sé ócam an phríosúin
Go bhfága sú an ghráin eorna na hÓglaigh dá spíonadh.

Is osclaíodh dom an stór a raibh ócam thar maoil ann
Is thug mé lán mo ghabhlach liom, mo dhóthain go ceann
   míosa,
Is nach mise a bhain gáire as an ngarda a bhí i mo thimpeall
Nuair a d'fhiafraigh mé den cheannfort cé air ar fhás an
   fianach
Is randa dideloram 'sé ócam an phríosúin
Go bhfága sú an ghráin eorna na hÓglaigh dá spíonadh.

7   Grew, BD (Major) (1958) *Prison Governor*. London: Herbert Jenkins (P.49).
8   https://lyricstranslate.com/en/%C3%B3cam-phr%C3%ADos%C3%BAin-prison-oakum.html-0

(I praise the juice of the barley for ever and ever
But isn't it a pity King George hunts those who make it
The Magistrate Seán Forde set an example for the people
By sending me to prison, to pick oakum
Randa didelorum, it's the prison oakum
That's in store for the young ones drinking poitín.

(They opened a storeroom overflowing with oakum
And I took with me an armful that would last me a month
But I set the guards around me laughing at me
When I asked the warder who had let the fur grow on it
Randa didelorum, it's the prison oakum
That's in store for the young ones drinking poitín.)

John Sarsfield Casey felt that, 'Plotting was the natural consequence of the isolation we were detained in … necessity is the mother of invention and so it was that all our thought was directed [to the problem of] in what manner might a channel of communication be opened'. Channels of communication, or *lines*, are among the means by which republican prisoners have always kept their struggle alive while in captivity, finding ways to subvert the jail system. Opportunities were identified and acted upon. The 'necessities', which the prison needed to supply, were quickly repurposed, and Casey and his comrades began using toilet paper as a medium of communication.

'Each prisoner is furnished weekly with a supply of brown tissue paper for WC [water closet: toilet] purposes. Letters and words might be formed by pricking the paper with a needle and holding it between you and the light; the words then became quite intelligible.' Casey believed that 'this was the best system invented as no notice whatever was taken of that paper by the warders, though they repeatedly handled such papers covered with several scraps of news.'[9]

The skill of pin-pricked communication in prison continued long after the1860s. In 1879, while carrying out a study of prison conditions, FW Robinson wrote of the women prisoners in Woking Jail writing to each other via 'Prison "stiffs", i.e., communications … pass from hand to hand till they reach the person for whom it is intended, and odd and ingenious are still the means by which they correspond. Failing ink or

9   John Sarsfield Casey (2005) *The Galtee Boy.* Dublin: University College Dublin Press (P.160).

a fly-leaf from the library books, a woman will secure at times a scrap of brown paper from the work-room or elsewhere, and prick with a pin on it all that she has to communicate. Ingenuity can hardly further go.'[10]

The toilet paper in prison, of course, was of a texture more akin to tracing paper than tissue and the same paper provided a communications lifeline a century later in Crumlin Road Jail in the 1950s, or in Armagh Prison and in the H-Blocks of Long Kesh in the 1970s. Plus ça change, plus c'est la même chose.

The prison prayer books provided another source of material. Flyleaves would be carefully torn from these books. A scrap of lead scraped from the water pipes in the toilets was used as a pencil.

These pencil dispatches were thrown across the dividing wall of the exercise cage when an opportunity presented itself or (were) carried around inside the clothing. However, 'as we were liable to be stripped naked several times daily the dispatches were secreted in some nook or blackened on the outside with black lead and cast on the floor, where it would require sharp eyes to distinguish it from the shining black flags.'[11]

Soon, however, the prisoners discovered a third system of telegraphy, 'to meet the increasing demands for news, plots, etc'. Their prison boots were oiled weekly, to keep the leather moist. This left the surface 'soft, greasy and easily impressionable'. Casey and his comrades cut the tongue from their boot or shoe, 'and with a pebble or a bit of slate (quantities of which lay on the ground of the exercise ring) any sentences may be written; and when read, by rubbing the hand across the leather these marks were completely effaced, and made fit for new "type".'[12]

It was a resourceful form of communication, the leather 'newspaper' or 'telegram' would be thrown from segment to segment of the exercise cage. The prisoners, unsure of who was walking in the passageway beside them on any given day, would firstly throw a pebble over with the question, 'Who?' and if the response thrown back confirmed that it was one of their comrades, the passing of the leather tongue would commence, with the prisoners always on the alert for the patrolling screws. In the same fashion prisoners would sometimes scrape news out onto the 'timber medal' which they were compelled to wear around their necks and these, too, would be utilised in passing news along.

10   https://blog.britishnewspaperarchive.co.uk/2021/04/15/exploring-life-behind-prison-bars/ (accessed 8-8-2023).
11   John Sarsfield Casey (2005) *The Galtee Boy*. Dublin: University College Dublin Press (P.160).
12   John Sarsfield Casey (2005) *The Galtee Boy*. Dublin: University College Dublin Press (P.161).

Casey wrote: 'Some ingenious rebel amongst the last arrivals from Dublin carved upon the bricks of the dividing walls all scraps of news from Ireland.'[13] Unfortunately for Casey and his fellow prisoners the news was not good. The planned Rising had floundered, and while the outlook was not encouraging: 'the Hope that blooms eternal ... never forsook us.'

After a year in Pentonville John Casey was moved to Portland Prison where, for a while at least, the rule of silence was lifted during the hours of work when prisoners were at hard labour in the stone yard. The ever-resourceful Casey secured the post of prison altar boy and would liberate newspapers each week from the priest's box. Gaining access to a newspaper would not have been possible while he was in Pentonville. There, even the chapel was not immune from the general rule of isolation. Despite its purpose as a place of worship, prisoners were kept separate from each other, each prisoner locked in a separate stall, all facing forward towards the chaplain with no line of sight to any other prisoner and with lines of warders on each side ensuring compliance. Only when hymns were being sung could the prisoners utter a sound, but this too was an opportunity to pass news as they 'sang' their news while warders were unable to pinpoint any particular culprit breaking the rules.

Once appointed as altar boy Casey seized his chance. A mass-trunk was brought in weekly for the Sunday service with the sacred vessels wrapped in old newspapers for protection. Starved of news from the outside world, the scraps of newspapers smuggled from the chapel by Casey would be passed from cell to cell through tiny gaps in the heating pipes, and on reaching the last cell of the side of the wing would be smuggled and hidden in the WC. The use of the toilet was available on Sundays only, and it must be supposed that on Sundays there was no slop-out as on other days when the prisoners used the cell toilets.[14] The official government report on building specifications for the new Model Prisons stated that: 'the construction of the cells should prevent all communication between one prisoner and another ... further they should be fitted up with the means for Washing, and with other Conveniences, so as to render it unnecessary for a prisoner to quit his

---

13   John Sarsfield Casey (2005) *The Galtee Boy*. Dublin: University College Dublin Press (P.162).

14   Incredibly, cells in the mid- and late-nineteenth century were equipped with hand basins, running water and plumbed toilets. Conditions deteriorated over the years. The degrading practice of 'slopping out' was finally brought to an end in prisons in Ireland in 2023, while in November 2023 almost 7,000 cells in Britain's prisons did not have toilet facilities with hundreds of prisoners still forced to use cell buckets.

The Hougoumont in which the last of the Fenians were transported

cell, excepting for attending Chapel and for Exercise.'[15]

Casey recalled: 'A *post-office* was established between the two boards of the bench into which the paper was placed. In the space of an hour or so everyone at the opposite side required to go to the closet. The last man destroyed the document. Hundreds of times the plan was used and never detected,'[16] until one day Casey was informed that he could no longer be in the sacristy alone, thus ending his access to the treasure trove of newspapers. The prison chaplains were no friends of the republican prisoners and would have had no compunction reporting the newspaper going missing from the trunk. Once again Casey and his comrades were cut off from news of the outside world. Before long, more challenging prison conditions were, literally, looming on the horizon.

The Wild Goose

It is possible that the first recognisable republican prison *newspaper* was published on board the prison ship Hougoumont while it was on route for Australia in 1867-68. The Hougoumont, built in 1852, had been named after the fortified Château d'Hougoumont which was

15   *Report of the Surveyor-General of Prison on the Construction of Pentonville Prison,* (1844) London: HMSO (P.12).

16   John Sarsfield Casey (2005) *The Galtee Boy*. Dublin: University College Dublin Press (P.192).

crucial to the British victory at the Battle of Waterloo. The Fenian prisoner Denis B Cashman was serving a seven-year term of penal servitude for a treason felony conviction. He was one of sixty-two political prisoners[17] among several hundred convicts on board the ship. His diary records the story of the ship's paper. Cashman, who was born in 1842, joined the Fenians at the age of sixteen and eventually became Head Centre for Waterford in the 1860s. He was editor and designer of the prison 'newspaper', which was handwritten on foolscap sheets of paper. The sheer endeavour and spirit of the Fenian prisoners was nothing if not inventive and creative when it came to sharing—and creating—news.

One of Cashman's fellow editors of the newspaper was the aforementioned John Sarsfield Casey who, like Cashman, kept a diary of the journey and what life on board the convict ship was like. Casey was four years younger than Cashman but no less active in the Fenians. He was transported at the age of twenty-one.

The prisoners left England on 12 October 1867 from the Isle of Portland on their ninety-day trip to Fremantle, Australia, arriving on 9 January 1868. It is worth recalling that on 23 November, 1867, while these prisoners were on their way to Australia, that the Manchester Martyrs, William Philip Allen, Michael Larkin and Michael O'Brien were publicly hanged at 8 am on a scaffold outside the walls of Salford Jail. The Fremantle prisoners were the last group of Irish prisoners to make that terrible journey as transportation to the penal colonies was coming to an end. The transportation consisted of both 'civilian' and 'military' Fenians who were quartered together and so had contact for the first time, since they had been assiduously held separately after their arrests. 'Military Fenians' were subjected to much harsher conditions in the English prisons before transportation. They were considered as more dangerous and treacherous because they had been organising from within the British military and were deemed highly treasonable. The treatment of all the Fenian prisoners on the ship, however, was in marked contrast to that meted out to non-political convicts on board. There were some two hundred convicts, who had very few rights and were often chained and held in close confinement. They were subject to a variety of physical punishments, including flogging, being placed on reduced rations and being locked in a small box-like cell, on deck, in the sweltering heat. The Fenian prisoners had much more liberty on board and their treatment was tolerable.

17   Cashman, Denis B (2001) (Ed. CW Sullivan III) *Fenian Diary* Dublin: Wolfhound Press (P.15).

The three diaries kept by prisoners on board (Denis B. Cashman[18], John Sarsfield Casey[19] and Thomas McCarthy Fennell[20]), combined with a complete set of the newspaper produced by the prisoners, *The Wild Goose,*[21] gives some idea of conditions during the journey. Life on board—despite the often-terrible weather and storms, seasickness, and poor rations—was a huge improvement over conditions in Pentonville and Portland. Where silence had been the order of the day in those prisons, now the prisoners could converse freely, hold nightly concerts and, in place of furtive communication scraped on the leather boot-tongues or pricked into toilet paper, they could in fact produce the ship's newspaper with materiel supplied by the prison chaplain.

On 25 October 1867, Casey wrote: 'Passengers relieving monotony of voyage by various games such as chess, dominoes, drafts, cards, dice etc. Evening enlivened by music (the banjoe [*sic*]) on deck accompanied by singing and dancing.'[22] On 31 October he wrote: 'Meeting about project about starting a newspaper whilst on board. J Duggan, Chairman; Mr John Flood appointed Editor; Mr J O'Reilly, Sub Editor; Mr C Keane, Reader; Mr D Bradley, Printer's Devil.'

According to Denis Cashman's diary those in attendance at the first meeting also included Con Mahony, Michael Coady, Joseph Noonan and himself, and also Kelly who was appointed Manager. The meeting was adjourned without having reached agreement on a name for the paper but a few days later—'after several beautiful suggestions'— Cashman reported that Kelly's proposal of *The Wild Goose* had been accepted.

Cashman took on the task of creating a masthead.

'The first number is to appear on Sat'y the 9th so I must go at the heading (a wreath of shamrocks with the name peeping thro' it). I expect to be rather busy for the voyage at it.'[23]

18   Cashman, Denis B (2001) (Ed. CW Sullivan III) *Fenian Diary* Dublin: Wolfhound Press.
19   https://catalogue.nli.ie/Record/vtls000575135 – John Sarsfield Casey: Journal of a voyage from Portland to Fremantle on board the convict ship Hougoumont, ed. Martin Kevin Cusack. National Library of Ireland original manuscript: MS 49,664/1
20   https://catalogue.nli.ie/Record/vtls000575127 – Thomas McCarthy Fennell: 'Life on a Convict Ship' or 'Misery of Penal Exile'.
21   'The Wild Goose: A Collection of Ocean Waifs.' A weekly newspaper issued on board the convict ship Hougoumont; ed. by J. Flood and John Boyle O'Reilly. Vol. 1, no. 1-7, (9 Nov. – 21 Dec.), 1867, New South Wales State Library, MLMSS 1542 (Safe 1/409).
22   https://catalogue.nli.ie/Record/vtls000575135 - John Sarsfield Casey (diary entry 25 October 1867).
23   Cashman, Denis B (2001) (Ed. CW Sullivan III) *Fenian Diary* Dublin: Wolfhound Press (P.72).

Casey noted in his diary that, 'the articles would be purely literary' in the newspaper. His diary doesn't record his views or any opinion on whether he agreed with that decision. These were very politically-motivated prisoners. The newspaper was not a secret project; it required the use of paper held by the ship hierarchy and crew, so perhaps this definition of a 'purely literary' format was a way of bypassing an official ban on the journal. Despite the 'purely literary' mission, over the following two months the content was often nationalistic in the sentimental way of the mid-nineteenth century emigré.

In a droll wordplay the 'paper' was sub-titled, 'A Collection of Ocean Waifs,' and was handwritten in a clear and steady copperplate hand. The 'printer's devil' and others copied the paper. Surviving copies have several variants of handwriting and Cashman records that the captain and his officers all asked for copies to be made as souvenirs of the final edition (a double-sized, sixteen-page Christmas issue).

Issue 1 had two different handwriting styles in the editorial alone, which probably indicates scribes copying from an original. Cashman's masthead design with the wreath of shamrocks was used in each edition; but since each was hand drawn, no two were identical. A festive variant of the shamrock scroll was used for the final edition in December 1867.

While adopting a 'purely literary' approach, the front page in the launch issue placed the 'Wild Goose' in the context of 'contemplating the pilgrimage and pride of the Wild Geese of other days', and to console readers for the past and 'strengthen them for the future'. There could be little doubt for contemporaries who the 'Wild Geese of other days' were. This was their homage to Irish soldiers who had fought in the Habsburg Empire in the 1700s with the intention of returning some day to liberate their own country.

Some articles spanned from edition to edition in serial form: the series *Queen Clíodhna and the Flower of Erin* began in Issue 1, for example. Satire and humour were frequently used among the contributions. In an article entitled 'The Markets', the lack of tobacco, a perennial prison problem, was bemoaned: 'Tobacco not to be had at any price; holders unwilling to part with the commodity.'[24] Other commodities mentioned included 'preserved potatoes and plum duff', which was a staple of the journey; port; inferior quality water (which was scarce); biscuit, chocolate, and oatmeal. The weekly editorial, always dated, ran under the strapline: 'They'll come again when south winds blow', aspiring no doubt for the return to Ireland from the southern hemisphere.

The first issue also included a personal account by 'JN' of an escape from custody aboard a train while en route to trial. It certainly stretched the notion of a purely literary publication! Another article—tongue-in-cheek—gave information about Australia for the travellers but contained subtle political commentary, such as, that the continent 'was taken in possession of by the Government of Great Britain in accordance with that just and equitable maxim "what's yours is mine, what's mine, my own".'[25] For the colonisation of Australia, read Ireland.

Other comments mentioned British officials securing annual salaries of £1,000 per year for life 'for enduring the fatigues of office for twelve months'. Ireland, on the other hand, was a place to be proud of: 'never, never, or rarely indeed, has our fair little country produced a degenerate son. No, no—wild, volatile, thoughtless, reckless, we may be called, but that stigma is undeserved.'

The paper provided a platform for both established and upcoming Fenian writers, including the deputy editor John Boyle O'Reilly who published poetry under his own name in every issue. Some writers preferred to use pen names like Laoi, Binn Éadair, Suir, or Boyne. Binn Éadair[26] was as prolific as O'Reilly, sometimes penning two or three poems in a single issue.

Other articles which appeared discussed Irish Folklore; the story of Lord Edward Fitzgerald; celebrating the Fourth of July in the USA; a letters column (with clearly fictitious correspondence); the occasional short piece ending in a pun; and reports on the ship's progress with statistics of longitude and latitude and daily distance travelled.

24   The Wild Goose Issue 1 (P.3).

25   The Wild Goose Issue 1 (P.8).

26   CW Sullivan identifies Binn Eadair as John Flood, Suir as Denis Cashman and Laoi as Edward Kelly. Cashman, Denis B (2001) (Ed. CW Sullivan III) *Fenian Diary* Dublin: Wolfhound Press (P.52).

In the final edition, contributors, aware that the voyage was nearing its destination, offered some thoughts on the future and the lives that lay ahead of the prisoners:

> The end of your uneventful but rapid passage quickly approaches, and already your hearts are beginning to quicken with anticipation at what may be your future in the new land you are fast nearing. I know not what may be in store for you: I cannot pierce the inexorable veil of the future—drawn alike for me and you; but on bidding you a long farewell, most likely, however we may wish it, never to meet again, I say to you—
>
> Courage, and trust in Providence. You have in your keeping things the most precious to the heart of man—things that no power can wrest from you, no matter whether your position be that of convicts, exiles, or freemen—your own honour—further to preserve unsullied; and remember, that the honour of any one is not a thing belonging to him alone, to be kept bright or stained at pleasure; but that the honour of each is the honour of all—a sacred trust, which it is your duty to keep pure and untarnished.[27]

The words of advice ring true through the ages and indeed there are echoes of 'the thought that says, "I'm right"'—so brilliantly evoked more than one hundred years later by Bobby Sands in his poem 'The Rhythm of Time'.

The set of newspapers held in the John Mitchel Library, New South Wales, are from the papers of John Boyle O'Reilly. He, in fact, was the first of the prisoners to gain freedom.

O'Reilly escaped a year after arriving in Fremantle, Western Australia. He reached America where he continued writing and became editor of the Boston newspaper *The Pilot*. O'Reilly as a 'military Fenian' would not have benefitted from two amnesties his civilian comrades secured from the British government in 1869 and 1871. 'Military Fenians', or members of the British Army charged with seditious activities, did not qualify for amnesty or 'ticket of leave', a form of long-term parole available (after a period of good behaviour) to civilian Fenians.[28]

27 The Wild Goose Issue 7 (P.2).
28 Britain had been exporting prisoners to the colonies for more than a century and had

After 1871, a small group of military Fenians remained in prison, their health and sanity being eroded daily.

In 1874 one of the remaining prisoners, James Wilson, smuggled a heart-rending appeal to John Devoy in the US seeking the assistance of the Fenian-affiliated Clan na nGael with an escape plan. In a daring global operation, Devoy contacted O'Reilly and the wheels were set in motion for a rescue, an escape which brought six Military Fenians safely to New York on board a whaling ship, The Catalpa, purchased by the Clan as a guise for the escape. They escaped, firstly, from the prison colony and made their way to Rockingham, thirty kilometers south of Fremantle, where the whaling ship was moored in international waters.

In April 1876, more than ten years after their original imprisonment, six of those who had travelled to Australia on board the Hougoumont were successfully brought half-way round the world to freedom by the editor of their old convict-ship newspaper, John B O'Reilly.

It is worth noting that the Fenian prisoners were not the last Irish republicans held in Australian prisons. Between December 1917 and February 1919 nine Irish republicans were interned in Darlinghurst Jail, Sydney. WJ Fegan was interned first in December 1917, followed by W MacGuinness, A Dryer, E McSweeny, M McGing, T Fitzgerald, F MacKeown and M Dalton in the middle of June 1918; and a few weeks later their number increased to nine with the arrest of M Kiely. Their surnames say it all. They were accused of being members of Sinn Féin and of the Australian division of the Irish Republican Army. With the end of the Great War their internment under regulations similar to the Defence of the Realm Act in Ireland came to an end, with seven of them being released in December 1918 and the other two freed in January and February 1919.[29]

---

been developing a practice where prisoners destined for transportation would serve an eighteen-month sentence in the Separate System in Pentonville Prison in preparation for the journey. There, they would be classified, and, as the Commissioner of the prison J.R.G. Graham wrote in 1842, the prisoner would be given the certainty that he was bidding adieu to his life in England and that only three options lay before the exile: 'He will be sent to Van Diemen's Land and if he behave well, at once to receive a ticket of leave, which is equivalent to freedom; if he behave indifferently ... to receive a probationary pass which will impose galling restraints on his liberty; and if he behave ill he will be transported to Tasman's Peninsula, deprived of liberty—an abject convict. *Report of the Surveyor-General of Prison on the Construction of Pentonville Prison* (1844) London: HMSO (P.50).

29   https://www.militaryarchives.ie/collections/online-collections/bureau-of-military-history-1913-1921/reels/bmh/BMH.WS1526.pdf (P.67).

CHATHAM PRISON

In 1858 O'Donovan Rossa, business manager of *The Irish People*, was imprisoned. After his release he was again arrested in 1865, was charged with treason felony and sentenced to penal servitude for life in England. In a by-election in 1869 he had also been elected MP for Tipperary South, but was disqualified because of his conviction. Rossa's treatment in Chatham Prison defies belief at times in the barbarity of the prison governor's attempt to break his will. This unbreakable Fenian spent long periods in the punishment cells, deprived of light, in total isolation, his hands cuffed behind his back for periods of up to thirty-four days on a bread and water diet and forced to eat from the floor.

The Surveyor General of Prison, Major J. Jebb, had noted as far back as 1844 in his report on Pentonville Prison that: 'Solitary confinement may be designated imprisonment without Labour or Employment, and it cannot legally be enforced for more than one calendar month at a time, nor for more than three months in a year.'[30] Almost a hundred years later the prison governor B.D. Grey was to write: 'I have never found that an unco-operative prisoner becomes more amenable after a bread-and-water diet. I never saw a man who appeared anything but impenitent and resentful when the punishment was over'.[31] Even with this knowledge, however, the British penal system threw everything they could at Irish republican prisoners.

O'Donovan Rossa was amnestied in 1871 on condition that he leave Britain and Ireland and go into exile. He went to the United States, joined Clan na Gael and the Fenian Brotherhood and established the newspaper *The United Irishman* which advocated a bombing campaign in Britain.

---

30   *Report of the Surveyor-General of Prison on the Construction of Pentonville Prison* (1844) London: HMSO (P.37).
31   Grew, BD (Major) (1958) *Prison Governor*. London: Herbert Jenkins (P. 49).

In 1883, a mere seven years after the Catalpa Rescue of the Fenian prisoners in Australia, an Irish republican called Tom Clarke was sentenced to penal servitude for life at London's Old Bailey. Clarke had been on the run in the USA after escaping from Ireland in the wake of an RIC man being wounded in a shooting in Tyrone. In America he had been active in Clan na nGael. The Irish Republican Brotherhood (IRB) and the Clan were planning a dynamite campaign advocated by the exiled O'Donovan Rossa, and Clarke was one of the *dynamitards*, ready to carry out the campaign. The British Government once again set out to create a regime in its penal institutions which would break republican prisoners both physically and mentally—just as they had tried to break Rossa earlier, during his imprisonment in the 1860s.

Clarke's *Glimpses of an Irish Felon's Prison Life* is as commanding a read as O'Donovan Rossa's *Irish Rebels in English Prisons*. The two prison memoirs are set less than twenty years apart, with Clarke suffering much of the same torment as his comrade in struggle. Perhaps Clarke is considered to be an 'old' prisoner because most of the images used of him, depict him in later life, but even at the time of his execution in 1916 (he was honoured as the lead signatory to the Proclamation) he was only fifty-eight. He had spent fifteen years in prison between 1883 and 1898 and had been free for eighteen years by 1916.

Clarke was a young man, twenty-three years old, when imprisoned, and full of energy, wiliness, fun, and a sheer determination not to be broken. He, in fact, often turned the prison regime upside down in finding ways to subvert the inhumane rules and conditions under which he was held. The mental health of two of his comrades, Thomas Gallagher and Alfred Whitehead, was irreparably broken by the prison system. Yet Clarke wrote: 'It must not be thought that Gallagher and Whitehead received any worse treatment than the other prisoners. By no means. Generally speaking, we were all treated alike, for the authorities deliberately set themselves to drive us all mad or to kill us, and they succeeded in doing this with most of our number.'[32]

His dogged will and ideology, that inner thought and belief in the right of his cause was what kept him going: 'Some of us realised this situation early in our imprisonment and saw that the mercilessly savage treatment was meant to smash us, and three of us, Daly, Egan and myself, deliberately set ourselves to defeat the officials' design.'[33]

32   Clarke, Thomas J. (1922) *Glimpses of an Irish Felon's Prison Life.* Dublin: Maunsell and Roberts (P.22).

33   Clarke, Thomas J. (1922) *Glimpses of an Irish Felon's Prison Life.* Dublin: Maunsell and Roberts (P.22).

Clarke and his comrades John Daly and James Egan were under no illusions as to the challenge. He described it as a 'fight against frightful odds' against 'the prison authorities, with all the horrors of their prison machinery, relentlessly striving to accomplish their objects with unlimited ways and means at their disposal.' The prisoners were 'each standing alone and friendless, but resolved never to give in, with nothing to sustain him in the fight but his own courage and the pride he had in being an Irish Fenian'. Once again, it was the *undauntable thought*:

> Throughout the whole time we stood loyally by each other … in close and constant communication with each other. Never a week passed but I received a voluminous note from John Daly—and some weeks two or three notes—and he received the same from me. This went on for about eleven years. As with Daly, so with Egan, for the eight years he was with us. Tell that to the prison authorities and they would say it was utterly impossible. But we, too, had reduced our business to a scientific system—it was diamond cut diamond. At all events they never had the satisfaction of catching notes with either of us.[34]

Those weekly communiques were to become their newspaper: 'Egan's notes would sometimes be illustrated with comic sketches, and they used to afford me many a chuckle and quiet laugh in the corner of my cell. At Christmas time we all wrote verses to each other—verses more treasonable perhaps than poetic.'[35] In Daly's notes to Clarke he 'Had taken to writing in newspaper style, using the editorial "We" on all occasions'.[36]

The unflappable Clarke was always devising systems of communication with the outside world, garnering news, and sharing this with his comrades. While in Portland Prison (the same prison from which the sixty-two Fenians had been transported to Australia twenty years earlier), he was sent to work in the tinsmith shop to make 'oil bottles, canisters and various kinds of tinware'. In time he was moved outdoors from the workshop proper to the storage yard to pack the finished items. At first he had no idea where the finished goods were going but soon he noticed that the same crates would be returned, empty,

---

34   Clarke, Thomas J. (1922) *Glimpses of an Irish Felon's Prison Life.* Dublin: Maunsell and Roberts (P.23).

35   Clarke, Thomas J. (1922) *Glimpses of an Irish Felon's Prison Life.* Dublin: Maunsell and Roberts (P.23).

36   Clarke, Thomas J. (1922) *Glimpses of an Irish Felon's Prison Life.* Dublin: Maunsell and Roberts (P.37).

after each delivery. He learned that the containers and bottles were being sent to the Royal Navy, via the Admiralty HQ in Woolwich Arsenal. With the assistance of his comrade John Daly (working in the carpenter's shop) a thin lath of wood was made up and painted black using the paint supplied for stencilling the wooden crates. Clarke then chalked a plaintiff message on the black board 'comm' for whoever would open the box, saying: 'For God's sake throw in a piece of newspaper, any old newspaper and earn the gratitude of a long term convict.'

The maxim 'any port in a storm' seems apt, and Clarke had decided to take a chance on someone in the old enemy, the Royal Navy, coming to his aid. The lath was placed in Container 24 and the box was dispatched. In due time the box returned and when he opened it, the box was full of newspapers. He successfully concealed the papers for days on end until he, Daly and Egan could share the treasure trove of news from the outside world. The prisoners, it must be remembered, were denied all access to news for years and one can imagine the excitement and sense of victory Clarke experienced in obtaining the consignment of illicit papers:

'I at once set to work at securing the newspapers. I got into the case, caught up a small bundle of the papers and secured them inside my waistcoat, then gathered up a bundle of the wet packing, holding that in my arm so as to conceal the lump under my waistcoat, got out of the case and over to the shed, and from behind the timbers arranged the packing to dry, and at the same time concealed the papers; then made another journey back and forwards, and kept on repeating this until I had all the papers in safety. Day by day for a long time after this I examined portions of the papers, that is, I would take some papers with me when going to the closet and look through them. On discovering a "newsy" bit I would, after reading it, tear it out and take it back with me to be put in concealment in order to be passed on to Daly later. From this time onwards newspapers of various kinds kept coming into me in fairly good numbers, and what a heavenly break it was on the hideous monotony of convict prison life!'[37]

Tom eventually set up a line of communication with comrades outside the prison through the friendly sailor he had never met, but eventually

37   Clarke, Thomas J. (1922) *Glimpses of an Irish Felon's Prison Life*. Dublin: Maunsell and Roberts (P.46).

that line too came to an end when, just as he was beginning to hatch an escape plan and had started to use code in his communications, he was moved unexpectedly from the tinsmith's yard. It was just one more obstacle to overcome.

The Irish Felon

It was in Chatham Prison, during the worst days of the regime there, that Tom had one of his most satisfying and subversive actions against the prison system. It was, he wrote, the first and only time that he edited a newspaper and ironically it was while he was working as a stereotyper in the printer's shop printing official prison forms that the idea came to him to give his friend Daly something to smile about. He knew that it would be 'a difficult thing to attempt under the eyes of the five officers in the shop, who had me, as an Irish prisoner, singled out for special surveillance, and it had to be carried through without arousing the slightest suspicion.'

Tom began by 'making a pie' of a task he had to print, by loosening the quoins or wedges in the printing typeface and spilling it on purpose. When he was given leave to collect more typeface, instead of returning the old type to the cases he hid the type away for further use.

'I worked at my paper at every odd moment I could, and it was only occasionally I could get a few minutes unobserved, and after eight or nine days I got it up after sundry accidents and close shaves of being detected. The next difficulty was to get it printed, for each machine and press in the shop had men working round it, and I had to be just as careful of them as of the officers, for they would have been only too glad to give me away to curry favour'.[38]

After some consideration of the problem, he turned to his stereotyper's oven, an apparatus closely resembling a letter-copying press.

'I placed my first page on the bed of the oven, inked it, and laid the paper on the type, brought down the top plate, and applied the necessary pressure. It printed beautifully, and in turn each page of my newspaper was printed off. It was on tissue paper, because ordinary paper would have been too bulky to escape the everlasting searches.'[39]

38 Clarke, Thomas J. (1922) *Glimpses of an Irish Felon's Prison Life*. Dublin: Maunsell and Roberts (P.38).

39 Clarke, Thomas J. (1922) *Glimpses of an Irish Felon's Prison Life*. Dublin: Maunsell and Roberts (P.39).

The following Sunday he delivered the 'newspaper' to his comrade Daly, whose 'coughing and chuckling in his cell that evening told me how he was enjoying it.' It was a newspaper without news, on tissue paper but it could easily have been taken for a paper from the outside world.

'In capitals on the top of page one was the name 'The Irish Felon,' and under that in small capitals came the information: 'Printed and Published at Her Majesty's Convict Prison, Chatham, by Henry Hammond Wilson'.[40]

Clarke's leading article was 'as treasonable as a leading article could be'. The next page purported to be news and was followed by an essay on prison philosophy. He even had one page illustrated, with woodcuts of convicts who had escaped from prison, and whose portraits had appeared in the *Hue and Cry*.[41]

'A couple of the most villainous looking of these pictures, with "criminal bumps" and all that, were made to stand for the infamous Sadlier and Keogh,[42] and served as pegs upon which to hang the story of these renegades' base betrayal.'

Another page contained an 'interview' with a Greek philosopher who 'when interviewed by the representative of *The Irish Felon*, had a great deal to say about England's Prison System—very little of it complimentary'.[43] And, of course, there was a poet's corner where Tom Clarke dedicated some verse to 'Pontius Pilate' (the prison governor, Captain W. Vernon Harris):

> The song I'll sing
> In the air will ring,
> Of Pontius Pilate O!
> That thundering thief,
> Our Chatham chief,
> The grunting dog you know.[44]

---

40 Tom Clarke had been arrested under the alias Henry Hammond Wilson, a supposed American businessman, and for years afterwards was referred to by friend and foe alike as 'Wilson'.

41 The *Hue and Cry*, more formally known as the *Police Gazette* was a newspaper published monthly between 1772 and 2017 with information of crimes and criminals the police were in pursuit of.

42 William Keogh and John Saidleir were two nationalist MPs who in the 1850s deserted the party to take high office under the British Crown (Keogh becoming a judge and responsible for the severe sentences imposed in the Fenian Trials of 1865-66). The names of Saidleir and Keogh remain a by-word for treachery.

43 Clarke, Thomas J. (1922) *Glimpses of an Irish Felon's Prison Life*. Dublin: Maunsell and Roberts (P.40).

44 Clarke, Thomas J. (1922) *Glimpses of an Irish Felon's Prison Life*. Dublin: Maunsell and Roberts (P.40).

The flimsy tissue paper, like so many of the hundreds of communiqués passed between Daly, Egan and Clarke, week in, week out, was never found, or at least, never found in a way which could be read. Clarke wrote:

> There were perforated iron ventilators built into the walls of our cells, and these masked horizontal air shafts. They formed very convenient wastepaper receptacles, for anything pushed through the ventilators dropped down a foot or so into the air shaft and could not be seen.
>
> The prison authorities knew that somehow we were able to carry on a clandestine correspondence. This they were aware of from their having captured a few notes by accident. Finally, they thought of the ventilator in the cells, and so ventilators were torn down and many buckets full of material taken out. It was carefully, very carefully examined, but all to no purpose, for not a single note was ever put into the ventilators without first being put into the mouth and reduced to pulp by rolling it between the hands.[45]

Not a trace remains of *The Irish Felon* today, except in the pages of Tom Clarke's memoir, *Glimpses of an Irish Felon's Prison Life*. Like *The Wild Goose* that preceded it, the *Irish Felon* was a digest without news but they both served a greater purpose than any newspaper. They raised morale, and validated the publishers, and the readers, as people apart.

Mosquito Press

Tom Clarke's return to the outside world in 1898 was to a life profoundly changed in political terms from the early 1880s when he was first imprisoned. Centenary commemoration events were under way for the United Irishmen's 1798 Rising and organisations to promote a Gaelic way of life, sport, language were everywhere. The Gaelic Athletic Association (GAA), formed in 1884 (barely eighteen months after Clarke's trial in 1883) was already an openly republican body,

---

45   Clarke, Thomas J. (1922) *Glimpses of an Irish Felon's Prison Life.* Dublin: Maunsell and Roberts (P.27)

Samples of the *Mosquito Press*

having among its leadership IRB members and numerous registered hurling and football clubs which practically dovetailed with local IRB Circles (the military units on which the IRB was established).

Conradh na Gaeilge (often called the Gaelic League) was founded in 1893 and while its founder and president, Dubhghlas de hÍde, was promoting a non-political path the organisation was slowly being populated by republicans—and non-republicans too.

Between 1900 and 1907 Tom Clarke spent time in the USA, working with John Devoy and Clan na nGael on the newspaper *The Gaelic American*. He returned to Dublin on the instructions of Clan na nGael to re-establish the IRB and was co-opted to the Supreme Directory in the role of Treasurer. He, Seán Mac Diarmada and many who would lead the 1916 Rising joined Conradh na Gaeilge and began a slow process of politicizing the organisation, a strategy which was not widely welcomed even among some republicans of the period. Kathleen Clarke, Tom's wife, for example, wrote of her dislike of Cathal Brugha when Brugha objected to Clarke and others politicizing the language movement.[46] Even Pádraig Mac Piarais (who became a member of Conradh na Gaeilge in 1896 at the age of seventeen)—who is most associated with the merging of the cultural and political struggle in the lead-up to 1916—had still to make those connections in the first decade of the 1900s.

The obverse of this historic allegation that republicans had somehow damaged Conradh na Gaeilge by infiltrating it, is of course that the Redmondites were equally, if not more active—if however less successful in keeping control of the organisation to promote their own brand of politics.

In 1910 Clarke helped establish the paper *Irish Freedom,* which he sold from his shops in 75a Parnell Street and 77 Amiens Street. His subversive prison paper, *The Irish Felon*, would have fitted easily into the political milieu of the early twentieth century. One hundred years later Eilis Murphy wrote of the period:

'In 1916, the printed word was the dominant means of communication with newspapers, posters, fliers, postcards on every street corner. Guerrilla printing presses produced cheap, short-lived newspapers to disseminate their message—one that was anti-authoritarian and radical. These newspapers became known as the 'Mosquito Press' by the authorities. As soon as the authorities shut one down, another one took its place. Like mosquitos, these presses were small but left a stinging bite'.[47]

Republicans were to the fore in this biting mosquito press. Their publications were banned, renamed, sold, distributed in the effort to educate, inform, and politicise their members and their supporters against a highly pro-British established media. To take just one example of this, republicans had founded a local anti-conscription newssheet in Tyrone, remembered years later by Kevin O'Shiel: 'We called our little daily sheet *The Conscription News*; and underneath that title ran the legend, 'The paper with the smallest circulation but the greatest influence in Co. Tyrone.' The paper would be posted in the office

---

46   Clarke, Kathleen (1991) *Revolutionary Woman.* Dublin: The O'Brien Press (P.142).
47   https://www.eilismurphy.com/work/mosquito-press

window of the local GAA Club each day, next door to the RIC Barracks. 'Every hour of the day there would be anxious groups round our window reading the news in our "paper". The sheet always ended by advising the young men to go either next door to the police barracks, join up in the British Army and help Haig who was in sore need of aid, or come into our club and help Ireland to defend herself against Conscription.'[48]

In the same vein, writing in *The Four Glorious Years*, Frank Gallagher—using the nom de plume David Hogan, since as a civil servant at the time he was precluded from using his own name— recalled that in 1917:

> It was vital to get any means of reminding the people that there was censorship. Mainly the reminders were given through what was known as the Mosquito Press ... small, difficult to kill, and with a bite that was remembered. Though I forget to what periods they belonged I remember many names: *Old Ireland, New Ireland, Young Ireland, Honesty, The Republic, The Irish Nation, Irish Opinion, The Irish Volunteer, The Spark, The Voice of Freedom, Nationality, Scissors and Paste, The Watchword of Labour, An Saoghal Gaedhealach, The Voice of Labour, The Irishman, The Tribune, Liberator.* There were others, I am sure.[49]

Little wonder, then, that when the mass internment and widespread imprisonment began after the Rising, republican prisoners began producing their own 'newspapers' within the confines of the camps and prison walls, continuing with the politicisation but also providing 'news' and entertainment to the captive readership.

48   O'Shiel,   Kevin   (1959)   https://www.militaryarchives.ie/collections/online-collections/bureau-of-military-history-1913-1921/reels/bmh/BMH.WS1770%20Section%206.pdf (P.771).

49   Hogan, David (1953) *The Four Glorious Years.* Dublin: Irish Press Ltd (P.39).

FRONGOCH

Frongoch[50] led the way. Frongoch, at one time a thriving Welsh whisky distillery, was latterly a German POW Camp. In 1916 it was rapidly converted into a sprawling prison for Irish republicans rounded up in mass swoops after the Easter Rising. The German officer POWS were moved out, leaving only two or three of their ranks (being treated for tuberculosis) behind in the hospital. Irish prisoners selected for internment were moved by sea from Ireland and by train from prisons across England and Scotland to take their place.

Frongoch was, in reality, divided into two parts, the North Camp and the South Camp: the former consisting of prefabricated wooden huts and the latter of an old stone building, three huge stories high, rat-infested and totally unsuitable for holding prisoners but considered 'fit' for the Irish internees.

The vast number of prisoners, (around 1,800 in total) in Frongoch meant that this incarceration was not going to resemble in any way the restrictive imprisonments inflicted on prisoners like Rossa, and Clarke in the 1800s. The empowerment given by numerical strength, and indeed the confidence of having risen up against the British Empire a couple of months earlier in Dublin in April 1916, guaranteed that the prisoners would rapidly establish structures and behave as an army within the prison camp and its wire and walls. Organisation, the like of which was never experienced before, was speedily achieved. A 'civilian' camp council was quickly replaced by a military (IRA) camp leadership. This ensured the maximum level of rights and recognition for the prisoners, and which rapidly earned the camp the sobriquet of 'University of Revolution'. The political status of the prisoners was, in fact, dependent on establishing a structure through which the British Army jailers would formally communicate with the POWs.

---

50 Officially spelled Fron-goch (see Ebenezer, 2005) the Camp is more often referred to as Frongoch in Irish prison memoirs.

Three different newspapers were in circulation in Frongoch: *The Frongoch Favourite, The Daily Wire* and *The Daily Rumour.*

The Frongoch Favourite

Issues of *The Frongoch Favourite*, nos. 1 and 2, appeared on 17 and 19 August 1916. They were handwritten, on one side only, with short satirical or fanciful items of camp 'news'. The strap heading below the title boasted that the paper was 'Read by everybody in Frongoch except the Censor'. In typical prison paper fashion, Issue 2 began by thanking the 'numerous' (fictitious) people who had sent in letters of thanks and assuring them that 'like the Frongoch prisoners, we are here to stay'. The single sheet also contained a 'report' about a fire which had some satirical references to John Redmond, the Home Rule leader, leader of the National Volunteers and recruiting sergeant for the British Army in 1914. Another contribution consisted of a list of 'mottoes of the day' which included one from the Tailor's Shop: 'as you sew, so shall you rip', and from the Barber's Shop: 'cleanliness is next to Godliness'.

There were, in fact, two barbers in Frongoch: Sweeney Newell from Galway and James Mallon from Dublin who in later years would trade in Dublin as 'The Barber of Frongoch'. Mallon was considered one of the most important men in the camp by some accounts, as he claimed to have a cure for scalp disease. The 'newspapers' (*The Frongoch Favourite*, and another paper *The Daily Wire*) were pinned to a notice board in the Barbers' Shops[51] which would explain why the papers were single-sided productions. There is no record of how many copies were made of each issue.

The Daily Rumour

A third camp paper in Frongoch was *The Daily Rumour.* It was published in the boot-making shop. Frank Hardiman, a Galway Volunteer interned in Frongoch, remembered *The Daily Rumour* by the name *The Frongoch Rumour* and told the Bureau of Military History researchers that: 'We also had boot repairing and tailors' shops. Stephen Jordan of Athenry was in charge of boot repairing. Stephen appointed

---

51 Sean Ó Mahony suggests in *Frongoch University of Revolution*, that they were displayed in the Barber's Shop which was a hive of all activity and entertainment during the day. O'Mahony, Sean (1987) *Frongoch* Dublin: FDR Teoranta.

Dick Murphy of Athenry as his assistant. The only thing Dick knew about leather or boot repairing he got from what he wore on his feet. It was a gift to see Dick at work wasting government leather and he certainly didn't spare the hammer.'

The *Daily* or *Frongoch Rumour* was usually written on brown wrapping paper for the want of better paper and posted daily on the window of their workshop. The humorous writings were certainly good but anyone reading what they gave out as the 'gospel truth' would immediately conclude that the authors were the most 'beautiful brace of liars' it was possible to meet in a day's walk. Dick Murphy's jovial ways made him a great favourite among the prisoners, and he and others contributed to the 'Humours of Frongoch', which in no small way helped to lighten the troubles of many other prisoners.[52] By the end of August 1916, two thirds of the internees had been released and the ephemeral newspapers in all liklihood ceased production around the same time.

52   Frank   Hardiman   (1950)   https://www.militaryarchives.ie/collections/online-collections/bureau-of-military-history-1913-1921/reels/bmh/BMH.WS0406.pdf (P.19).

LEWES PRISON

While the prisoners in Frongoch 'enjoyed' political status large numbers of republicans arrested and charged after 1916 were sentenced to penal servitude, hard labour and long terms of imprisonment without political recognition. These prison sentences had been imposed in courts martial held in Richmond Barracks during May 1916 under emergency powers given to the military. Included in this category were prisoners who had been sentenced to death but had their sentences commuted to long terms of imprisonment. These 'convicts' were dispersed across a range of English and Scottish prisons. With the newly-found confidence from their numbers, and undoubtedly the knowledge and contradiction that thousands of their comrades, by a simple stroke of fate, were being held under very different conditions, they began immediately campaigning, with varying degrees of success, for rightful recognition as political prisoners.

(Fifty years later a similar contradiction in treatment and conditions would fortify prisoners, the men in the H-Blocks and the women in Armagh Prison's B Wing, in their battle to gain conditions equal to prisoners with special category status being held in the cages of Long Kesh and Armagh Prison's A Wing.)

The sentenced prisoners soon began flexing their muscle. They organised classes and lectures and their own 'mosquito press'. In Lewes Prison, around 130 republican prisoners were held (between spells in Maidstone and Pentonville). As fate would have it, their numbers included many gaeilgeoirí including Eoin MacNeill, Éamonn de Valera, Paraic Ó Fathaigh, Tomás Aghais, Colm Ó Gaora and others. MacNeill was under a cloud of distrust by many prisoners because of his sabotage of the Rising, but de Valera set about his rehabilitation by calling the POWs to attention in his honour on his first day in the prison.

Ó Gaora wrote of those days in Lewes in his memoir *Mise* and expressed some disappointment at 'daoine a bhí sa bpriosún liom agus a chuaigh i gcontúirt a n-anama ar son a dtíre, is nuair a chuireamar ranganna Gaeilge ar siúl sa bpriosún nach ndéanaidís oiread is iarracht ar fhocal den teanga a fhoghlaim. Ní hea go deimhin, ach chuaigh deascán acu ag foghlaim Gearmáinise, rud a chuir ionadh mór ormsa.' ('People who were in prison with me, who had risked their lives for their country, and yet when we established Irish classes they made no effort to learn the language. Indeed, more than that, some even took to learning German, something that really surprised me'.)[53]

An Bhuabhall

It was not all so bleak for the Irish language, however, despite Ó Gaora's frustrations. There were so many men amongst the Lewes Prison felons who had been working in the language movement prior to 1916 that they decided to set up a newspaper or magazine. It would all have to be done in a clandestine way, of course.

'I lámhscribhinn a bheadh an páipéar scríofa. Páipéar dhátheangach a bhí ann. Cheapamar eagarthóirí lena aghaidh. Ba é Páraic Ó Fathaigh fear na Gaeilge, agus Tomás Ághas an t-eagarthóir Béarla a bhí ina bhun. *An Bhuabhall* ab ainm dó.' (It was a handwritten manuscript, and bi-lingual. Páraic Ó Fathaigh was the man for the Irish and Tomás Ághas was the English language editor. We called the paper *An Bhuabhall* (*The Trumpet*).'[54]

Lewes Prison was the site of protest for political recognition by the sentenced republican prisoners and after some weeks they went on strike demanding segregation from non-political prisoners, and treatment as prisoners of war. They proceeded to wreck the prison. They were put in isolation and punished and in the process lost access to paper, with *An Bhuabhall* becoming collateral damage in the struggle. Another mosquito swatted; another paper gone—but in keeping with the mosquito analogy, another would soon take its place.

Many men, and a small number of women, were interned in scattered groups across the penal landscape of England, often in wings of prisons which had been rapidly emptied of their normal residents to make way for the Irish POWs. Besides Lewes, another group of

53   Ó Gaora, Colm (1969) *Mise*. Dublin: Oifig an tSólathair (P.168).
54   Ó Gaora, Colm (1969) *Mise*. Dublin: Oifig an tSólathair (P.169).

prisoners was held in Reading Jail. Reading Jail had been made infamous by the poetry of Oscar Wilde, a fact not lost on the newly-arrived Irish, some of whom noticed a small garden on their way from reception to their wing. Wilde's mother was the radical, nationalist poet Jane Wilde who wrote for the Young Ireland movement's paper *The Nation* under the pen-name Speranza.

'What astonished me most was the sight of flowers,' recalled Darrell Figgis, one of the first internees to arrive. 'Then some of us remembered the cause. One of the graves unlocked the secret. It was marked with the letters C.T.W.[55] and the date, 1896, to whom Oscar Wilde's 'Ballad of Reading Jail' had been inscribed, and in celebration of who's passing the poem had been penned.'[56]

Ernest Blythe arrived in Reading Jail via Brixton Prison. He, like Liam Mellows, had been banned from living in Ireland earlier in 1916 and was deported to England. Just before Easter 1916 Mellows managed to evade surveillance and with assistance from the IRB had escaped back to Ireland in time for the Rising where he led the Galway fight. Blythe was arrested in Abingdon and interned for the remainder of the year, firstly in solitary confinement and then separated from any other republican prisoners in Brixton. From July until December of 1916, he was held in Reading Jail.

'Ní mise an t-aon duine amháin ar chúis áthais dó bualadh leis an gcomhluadar a bhí i Reading',[57] he wrote. 'Ní raibh duine ar bith san áit an lá úd nach raibh díreach tar éis casadh le cairde nach raibh feicthe le míonna nó fiú cloiste uathu aige. I ngach ball is póirse bhí triúr nó ceathrar ag caint go bríomhar, agus ag malartú scéalta go gliondrach lena chéile'.[58]

The prisoners soon began organising. There was some dissent from the beginning as to who was in command of the prisoners. The writer Darrell Figgis with the support of Herbert Pim (an eccentric convert to republicanism who within two years would make one of several volte-faces in his life and become a unionist, pro-conscriptionist), was elected Officer in Command for a while. The leadership of the republican struggle was in transition: in Reading (as in Frongoch) the initial prison

---

55 Charles Thomas Wooldridge, a trooper of the Royal Horse Guards, hanged for killing his wife.

56 Figgis, Darrell (1917) *A Chronicle of Jails*. Dublin: Talbot Press (Chapter xviii).

57 de Blaghd, Éarnán (1973) *Gaeil á Múscailt*. Dublin: Sáirséal agus Dill (P.64).

58 'I wasn't alone in being delighted to meet the company in Reading. There was no-one among us that day who wasn't meeting up with friends that they hadn't seen or heard from for months. In every nook and cell doorway there were three or four talking animatedly and merrily swapping stories' (my translation).

leadership was in the hands of interned members of the political movement but the military leadership, the IRA forged in the Easter Rising, would soon take control of the jails. Figgis wrote:

The prison actually held only twenty-two cells. There was, in addition, a hospital, a maternity ward, and two padded cells, one permanent and one temporary. The hospital and maternity ward consisted of two cells each, with the intervening wall removed. In each of these, three men were placed (there being some little rivalry for the maternity ward), which with the use of the temporary padded cell provided for all of us. In addition to this, there was also an observation ward, on the ground floor, similarly constructed of two cells converted into one, and this was given to us as a recreation room. All these cells were on one side of the building, the other side being a blank wall, and the only light that came to the passage struggled down through skylights.[59]

In this confined space the British placed many who would become, in time, the leadership of republicanism. Many of these men died in prison or beyond the walls in the six years which followed. Reading Jail prisoners included Arthur Griffiths, Terry (Terence) Mac Swiney, Tomás Mac Curtain, Seán T O'Kelly, Peadar Ó hAnnracháin, Denis McCullough (President of the IRB in 1916), Piaras Mac Cana (who would die in prison), Pádraig Ó Máille, Cathal Shannon, Henry Dixon (who would become librarian in Frongoch and would have the dictinction of holding the same role in Ballykinlar Camp in 1921), Joseph McBride (brother of 1916 leader Major John McBride, executed a few months earlier), Liam Ó Briain, Dick McCormick and two other Irish Citizen Army members, Mac Gabhann and O'Neill.[60]

An Foraire

With so many intellectuals and gaeilgeoirí the prisoners created the first ever prison 'jailtacht' when the top third of the long dining table was designated as 'Irish only' during mealtimes.[61] It was little wonder that thoughts would soon turn to a wing newspaper as an outlet for their

59   Figgis, Darrell (1917) *A Chronicle of Cells*. Dublin: Talbot Press (Chapter xviii).
60   Possibly James McGowan and James O'Neill, both ICA members listed in Sean O'Mahony's Frongoch. O'Mahony, Sean (1987) *Frongoch* Dublin: FDR Teoranta.
61   de Blaghd, Éarnán (1973) *Gaeil á Múscailt.* Dublin: Sáirséal agus Dill (P.72).

creativity; and so *An Foraire* was established. Eamon O'Dwyer remembered that, 'amongst the things we got up to, there was a jail journal, and this was edited by Griffith, and the artist was Sean Milroy. Needless to say, with all those writers, it was very interesting.[62] (Milroy, a member of the Hibernian Rifles, a small armed body of nationalists who had joined with the Volunteers in the Rising, would also provide drawings two years later in 1918 in Lincoln Prison for another jail journal, *The Insect*, see below.)

Terence Mc Swiney was responsible for the handwritten weekly paper's name, although Arthur Griffiths was editor. The paper was different in so much as it was a bi-lingual paper from the beginning and since Griffiths could not write or speak Irish it fell to Peadar Ó hAnnracháin to contribute and edit the Irish language articles.[63] Ó hAnnracháin wrote both prose and poetry for the paper.

'Terence MacSwiney wrote every week,' recalled Blythe in his statement to the Bureau of Military History research. 'Peadar Ó hAnnracháin wrote an Irish contribution every week and read what he had written.' The prisoners read the paper aloud to a weekly wing meeting, a custom which was also practiced in other prisons. 'Griffith himself wrote every sort of thing in the journal. He wrote a very simple, very interesting series of articles about South Africa. He wrote mock heroic ballads. He also wrote, from time to time, detective stories which dealt with prison events and featured a detective named "Vidoc Brennan", who was identifiable with Michael Brennan.'[64] Brennan, who would later feature in protests in Dundalk Jail and in Belfast Prison, had been a member of the Supreme Council of the IRB and was arrested during Easter Week 1916 on his way from Clare to Galway where he was seeking to meet with Liam Mellows.[65] Griffith wrote humourous articles, poetry, song and despite the serious if not dour appearance conveyed by photographs of the time, he seems to have revelled in wing life and the sense of devilment that accompanied it, constantly whistling and revealing a deep knowledge of Irish tunes.[66]

Under the influence of Peadar Ó hAnnracháin, Blythe, too, began to write in Irish for the first time and one or two short articles of his

62   Eamonn   O'Dwyer: https://www.militaryarchives.ie/collections/online-collections/bureau-of-military-history-1913-1921/reels/bmh/BMH.WS1403.pdf (P.60).

63   de Blaghd, Éarnán (1973) *Gaeil á Múscailt.* Dublin: Sáirséal agus Dill, (P.79).

64   Ernest Blythe: https://www.militaryarchives.ie/collections/online-collections/bureau-of-military-history-1913-1921/reels/bmh/BMH.WS0939.pdf (P.70).

65   O'Farrell, Padraic (1997) *Who's Who in the War of Independence and Civil War.* Dublin: Lilliput Press.

66   de Blaghd, Éarnán (1973) *Gaeil á Múscailt.* Dublin: Sáirséal agus Dill (P.91).

were included in *An Foraire*. It would be good preparation for when, a year later, Blythe would edit the prison paper in Belfast's Crumlin Road Jail. Some of Blythe's prison articles would also be published outside the prison in *An tÓglach*, the IRA newspaper. *An Foraire*, also known by some of the prisoners as *The Outpost*, was one of the longest running and eclectic of the prison papers. 'Nearly everybody in the prison contributed to it from time to time,' said Blythe.

Reading Jail was a prison which never held more than thirty-eight republican prisoners, all of whom appear to have been hand-picked by the British because they had been identified as leaders of the political and military movement, language activists and prisoners. Some of these men had been sent to Reading from Frongoch as punishment for leading protests there when the prisoners took on the British camp commandant over work, conscription, and other issues. They felt, no doubt, as if they were in an outpost, separated from the bulk of the republican internees being held in Wales. But in Reading, prisoners were by all accounts in control of their lives by day and by night, so much so that it eventually led to complaints by Mathew Loan, the prison steward[67] to the British Home Office: '… the Irish prisoners gave us little peace and quiet between 7 pm and 10,' he wrote in his letter. 'There was shouting and cheering, drilling, chorus singing, violin and flute playing with step-dancing, besides much walking and running up and down stairs, all of which we heard evenings most plainly and which disturbed the peace and quiet I ought to have enjoyed after my trying day's due.'[68] He requested a transfer to a different prison but it appears he had to stick to his own 'outpost' until the prisoners were released in December 1916.

In an ironic twist the next time the title *Outpost* would be used in a prison paper was sixty years later in Magilligan Prison. On that occasion a periodical called *The Magilligan Outpost* was used not by republican prisoners but by loyalist prisoners. The content, as can be imagined, was not sympathetic to the republican cause.

---

67 A prison steward was in charge of purchases and provisions in the prison. It was a senior position and came with a house on the grounds of the prison, on a par with housing provided to the governors and chaplains.

68 https://www.irishpost.com/news/prison-steward-asked-moved-singing-dancing-easter-rising-prisoners-letter-reveals-87043

Prisoners on parade in Frongoch and prisoners arriving in Frongoch Camp

UNFREE PRESS
1917–1924

The East Wing, Kilmainham Jail, courtesy of Kilmainham Gaol Museum

'ROUGHS AND TOUGHS'

The last of the internees were released from Frongoch a couple of days before Christmas 1916 and the Reading Jail internees were freed on Christmas Eve. Those who had been deported from Ireland before the Rising were warned on being released from internment that the deportation orders were still valid and that if they returned to Ireland, they could face re-arrest. In fact, that is what happened to Blythe in 1917. He was arrested in Cork after discreetly living in his hometown of Lisburn for several months, although he had been aware that his arrest was always a possibility. After being imprisoned for breaching his deportation order, he went on hunger strike, as other prisoners were doing in Mountjoy. When the strike ended he was transferred to Dundalk Jail to serve out his one-year sentence.

Dundalk Jail was a two-winged prison, with each wing holding around one hundred republican prisoners who organised their own daily routine. The boredom was relieved by general boisterousness as two or three 'secret societies' formed in the wing. The secret clubs were in the style of 'The Black Hand' gang which had been behind much of the devilment a year earlier in Frongoch. While some of the more self-important prisoners looked on The Black Hand as a nuisance in Frongoch, and others thought that the group was a front for the IRB, the 'gang' was often in the front line in opposing and challenging their British jailers. In Frongoch, for example, when an attempt had been made to engage the internees in forced labour the Black Hand men quickly volunteered to report for the work. In the ensuing days they made the British plans unworkable through disruption and sabotage. In another stand-off the British commandant had ordered prisoners to carry out cleaning duties in the British army latrines and it was the Black Hand members who frustrated the British orders.

According to Blythe, in Dundalk prison these 'societies' adopted names like the wholly inappropriate Ku Klux Klan and the less offensive Sweeney's Roughs and Toughs.

'B'shin caitheamh aimsire nár bacadh leis in aon phríosún eile ina rabhas-sa,'[69] was Blythe's view of the 'bréagchumann' or 'pseudo-societies' which of course were not taken seriously. The prison paper, *The Truth* (see below), doesn't mention the former grouping at all, but mentions others such as The Harriers and The Bruisers. Frank Thornton remembered the rough and tumble (or rough-houses) that occurred:

> There was quite an assembly of well-known people in Dundalk Gaol at that particular period; Terry McSwiney, Sean Treacy, Mick Brennan of Clare, Mick Colivet of Limerick, Frank and Leo Henderson, Dick McKee, Dublin, Paddy Sweeney of Dublin, Ben Hickey of Tipperary, Oscar Traynor of Dublin, Dinnie Lyons of Kanturk, John Brady of Midleton, Tommy Foley from Kerry, Liam Malone of Westport, Tommy Ketterick of Westport, Charlie Gavin, Westport, Tom Hehir of Ennis, Joe Reid of Westport, Seamus O'Neill, Tipperary, Paddy O'Keeffe, Clare, T.P. Sullivan, Kerry, Jim Leddon of Limerick, Jim McInerney, Limerick, John O'Brien, Killaloe, Ernie Blythe, Diarmuid Lynch (Cork). Very soon after my arrival at Dundalk Gaol, elections were held, and an OC, Adjutant and General Staff to conduct the affairs of the prisoners were elected. Mick Brennan was elected OC. I was Adjutant, Terry McSwiney, Dick McKee, Sean Treacy, Frank Henderson, Oscar Traynor and Diarmuid Lynch were elected as staff. Inter-wing rivalry was encouraged, and it wasn't long until the Handball Championship of the prison was being fought out against the gable end wall of one of the wings. During the election for the various officers, election meetings were held by the supporters of the various nominees and some very rousing scenes took place when attempts were made by one side or the other to break up some particular meeting. The weapons used, in a lot of instances, were potato stalks which were secured from the garden.[70]

It was boisterous craic, and release of pent up energy. Sweeney's Roughs and Toughs, named after their leader Paddy Sweeney, decided at one point to produce their own prison newspaper. A surviving copy

---

69   de Blaghd, Éarnán (1973) *Gaeil á Múscailt*. Dublin: Sáirséal agus Dill (P.166). 'This was not a pastime I met in other prisons.' (My translation).

70   BMH WS0510: Frank Thornton (pp. 55-57).

of Vol. 1, No. 1 was edited by Seamus Ó Neill and carried the logo: 'Bíonn an Fhirinne Searbh i gConuidhe.'[71]

This journal was called *The Truth*. On each side were the words 'Rough' & 'Tough'[72] and, underneath, 'A Journal of uncommon sense'. The last copy of this journal to be issued was taken out by Long John Quinn, a prisoner who was released in 1918, and who was a linotype operator in the *Dundalk Examiner*. Quinn's first action on being released was to set up the last edition of this paper and he had about twenty copies printed.[73]

The Roughs and Toughs began composing stories, gathering wing tales, and altering the details; noting down odd words and phrases they had overheard among an unsuspecting prison population and so on. The finished product contained exaggerated accounts of battles between the Toughs and their nemesis, the Bruisers; poems praising—and occasionally parodying—the Toughs and their leaders. The verses also provide a useful historic record in so far as names of members of the Toughs are given: Traynor, Hickey, Ketterick, Sullivan, Thornton, Ring, Brady, Foley and others with some banter against the prison conditions, food, etc.

On a more serious note, an interesting Irish language article recounts how prisoner Diarmuid Ó Loinsigh managed to get married on a visit. The story of the marriage has become part of the lore of Dundalk Jail. Ó Loinsigh was about to be deported to the USA and asked for permission to get married to his fiancée, Kathleen Quinn. A sympathetic Dundalk priest arrived for a visit with a number of prisoners timed to coincide with a visit between the bride and groom to be. At a given signal, the priest moved to the couple while the other prisoners distracted the screws' attention and the deed was done. The witnesses signed the papers later that day and smuggled them out to be recorded by the Registrar:

THIS IS TO CERTIFY that it appears from the Register of Marriages in the Parish of Dundalk, that DIARMUID LYNCH and KATHLEEN M. QUINN were lawfully married in St. Patrick's Parish, Dundalk, according to the rite of the Catholic

---

71   HE:EW.579 Copy of 'The Rough Tough Truth'. A Journal of Uncommon Sense, Dundalk Jail, June 1918, Vol. 1 No. 1. Prison Journal—printed.

72   Coincidentally, the term 'RTP' or 'Rough, Tough, Provie', was used in banter among republican prisoners as late as the 1990s in Long Kesh and I wonder if, besides certainly a historic resonance, there is a subconscious historic link.

73   BMH WS0510: Frank Thornton (pp. 55-57).

Church, on the 24th day of April, A.D. 1918, the WITNESSES being MICHAEL BRENNAN and CARMELL QUINN. Officiating Priest: REV. A. RYAN. Marriage noted as contracted in a private place.

Blythe, it appears, was less than happy with the paper produced by the Toughs: so much so that he did not even record its name in his memoir. He sent a copy of the paper out to Méadhb Fitzgerald (wife of the IRA Director of Publicity, Desmond Fitzgerald) and her view of the publication was scathing,[74] even if the Roughs and Toughs were proud of their journal. 'She said that the publication was so stupid and childish that it nearly drove her mad. She never thought, she said, that men over the age of their teens—even in prison or internment camps—could be so foolish. She was disgusted, as she assumed any woman would be.'

A hundred years later we can only speculate if the paper as bad as she made out. Was Blythe being mischievous in any case, by sending a prison 'slag-sheet' out of the prison? Was Méadhb Fitzgerald too prudish and strait-laced? Frank Thornton was less prissy about the paper. He said: 'This journal, which was written by quite a number of us, was very voluble in its criticisms of the general appearances, actions, characteristics, etc. of each and every member of the prison, *but it was good fun.*'[75]

Whatever the problems of some strait-laced republicans with the paper, it was short-lived. The prison population in Dundalk soon dwindled and the final twenty-five or thirty prisoners, with their OC Michael Brennan, were moved to Crumlin Road Jail, and The Roughs and Toughs' paper came to an end.

The Dundalk prisoners arrived in Belfast to find the prison in a state of tension arising from a parcels strike. Many of the prisoners were grumbling about this strike, which was adhered to but not widely supported, particularly among the Dundalk prisoners. The strike eventually ended, although tensions had by now arisen between Austin Stack, the OC, and Michael Brennan, who had lost rank upon entering prison but was put forward as a spokesperson for the Dundalk prisoners, as if they were a separate entity in the wing. When the Vice OC, Eamonn Fleming, was released, fresh elections were held and Blythe was elected as the new Vice OC. He promptly introduced a regime that went against

74   de Blaghd, Éarnán (1973) *Gaeil á Múscailt.* Dublin: Sáirséal agus Dill (P.167).
75   BMH WS0510: Frank Thornton (pp. 55-57).

THE

Rough TRUTH Tough

Dionn an fpinne Seapó i gComnaire.

A JOURNAL OF UNCOMMON SENSE.

June 1918]   Dundalk Jail.   [Circulation Strictly Limited

VOL. I. NO. 1.   EDITED BY Seumar Ua Neill.   PRICE ONE PARCEL.

VIOLENT SCENES AT EXECUTION.

FEARFUL BLOODY FIGHTS.

SEVERAL KILLED AND INJURED.

On Friday while one Patk. O'Keeffe, who had been condemned to death by Sweeney's Toughs after the usual Courtmartial held the previous night—when O'Keeffe was found guilty of espionage—several of the Tough Gang entered the Circle, the gate being held by armed Toughs, who allowed none to enter without giving the pass-word. When O'Keeffe was being pinioned by the executioner, assisted by the President and Vice-President of our Executive—he resisted violently and inflicted several wounds on the executioner. The latter—like a true Tough —persisted in his duty, after which prisoner was conveyed to the Circle. There sentence of death was duly carried out. A scene of wild excitement then took place—when a considerable number of the Bruiser mob attacked our forces. The odds against the Toughs were 25 to 1, yet, with that courage and bravery worthy of the Toughs, the Bruisers were routed, leaving several killed and wounded on the field.

The success of this fight is due to the wonderful sagacity of President Sweeney, who personally directed the operations.

SPECIALS.

It is of absolute necessity that our secret oath be not divulged, and, to ensure that worthy object, we give it here:
By all the holes in Sweeney's socks,
By Traynor's unpatched trousers,
By the growth of Hickey's flowing locks
And Ring's death-dealing rousers,
By the face unwashed of Thornton Frank,
By Brady's boat-like boots,
By Kitterick—the Mayo Lank—
And the raskers Foley loots,
By Hehir, the quick-delivery man,
By Sullivan the crazy,
By Eustace—sturdy in the van—
And O'Neill, who is so lazy,
By all the names, I swear above,
To be a Tough for ever;
My duty I will never shirk—
Oh! never, never, never.
So help me—Margarine.

WHAT WE WANT TO KNOW.

(a) Do the all-powerful British statesmen intend to till the German Plot in Ireland this year?—and what sort of a crop do they expect?

(b) The Price and Age of the Cow that ran through the Soup on Thursday last?

(c) Does "Extra Fatigue" mean auditing the books and keeping the cash in the office?

(d) Who is the young lady that arouses such energy in the Commandant as to make him polish his gaiters when she visits him?

(e) Was the Deportation of Diarmuid Lynch necessary, as a war measure, to protect the Black Pig?

(f) Does a Spring Offensive bear any relation to a Spring Onion? Has unfavourable weather any effect—on its shooting?

(g) Why the occupant of No.7 A2 dresses his hair before and after meals? What Price Grace (grease)?

(h) Has the wearing of a grey trousers by one of our Councillors anything to do with the Governor getting a new suit?

(i) Why the Government treats its Blue Books as Scraps of Paper?

(j) Where Sweeney, Traynor and McKee will go after leaving here?

(k) Whether it is meat or whale-blubber is served for dinner twice a week?

(l) Do the mere mortals of this "Home", think they can get the better of Sweeney's Hooligans? It so—how?

(m) If the warders went out on strike would the prisoners be locked out?

By B.T.O.H.

EDITORIAL.

TO ALL WHOM IT MAY CONCERN.

In bowing to the public we make no apology for our appearance at this critical period in the history of our Organisation.

To give light and understanding where darkness and ignorance abound—to help towards the realisation of our objects, to foster a true spirit of brotherhood a la Sweeneiesc, to the overthrow of all secret societies, to report the progress of our organisation, the efficiency and activity of our members, the rectitude of our Executive—we hereby dedicate this Journal.

All communications to the Editor.

National Museum of Ireland

all he had promised in the run-up to the election when he had pledged to establish a more liberal culture in the prison. Once in his new role, he imposed a militaristic regime, thus annoying his prison comrades.

Jail Birds' Journal, Glór na Carcrach, Faoi Ghlas

Blythe had begun a newspaper on his arrival in Crumlin Road although his paper wasn't the only one in circulation in the prison at the time. Art O'Donnell recalled that the *Jail Birds' Journal* was promulgated by Seamus Murray of Dublin and Seamus McEvilly of Mayo, while Ernest Blythe edited a journal *Glór na Carcrach.* In each case one copy only was available, which the editor read standing on a bench in the laundry.[76] A paper named *Faoi Ghlas* was also produced during those years. Blythe modestly recalled that:

> *Glór na Carcrach* was, as far as I remember, pretty good. Kevin O'Higgins regularly contributed a serious article once a fortnight and a humorous article once a fortnight. Jim Burke also contributed regularly, and Terence MacSwiney contributed several songs and a number of serious articles. I generally did the leading article myself. One of my articles dealt with the question of facing the threat of conscription. A number of the prisoners thought the article was very good and asked for a copy of it. This copy was taken out of the prison by some man, whose term had expired, and handed in to Volunteer Headquarters. Apparently it was printed in *An t-Oglach*, and portions of it were later reproduced in Piaras Beaslaoi's book on Collins.[77]

Fionán Ó Loinsigh wrote in Irish for the paper while occasional contributors included Hubert Hunt, Andrias Ó Broin, Michael Kirby and an elderly prisoner by the name of McKenna who had spent time in the USA. Blythe also tried to replicate Griffith's style from the paper in Reading Jail by making news items out of small happenings in the wing. All in all, *Glór na Carcrach* lasted six months and the laundry would be full every Sunday with prisoners listening to the weekly reading of the paper.

Throughout 1917–1918 the British continued to arrest republicans in Ireland and Britain on charges of sedition, breaches of deportation orders and similar offences. The prisons became a battleground for political recognition and there were numerous hunger strikes, releases, re-arrests.

---

76   Art O'Donnell: https://www.militaryarchives.ie/collections/online-collections/bureau-of-military-history-1913-1921/reels/bmh/BMH.WS1322.pdf (P.36).

77   Ernest Blythe: https://www.militaryarchives.ie/collections/online-collections/bureau-of-military-history-1913-1921/reels/bmh/BMH.WS0939.pdf (P.109).

Crumlin Road Jail, 1918

Thomas Ashe, a 1916 leader, was arrested in August 1917 and sentenced to two years' hard labour. On 20 September he began a hunger strike against prison conditions, and during a forced-feeding five days later he died when the feeding tube entered his lung. Another hunger strike in Mountjoy ended with the release of the hunger strikers on health grounds—with the intention that they be re-arrested when their health improved. The Prisoners (Temporary Discharge for Ill Health) Act from 1913 which had been enacted to deal with the suffragettes' hunger strikes, had become known as the Cat and Mouse Act.

Conditions in the prisons were improved with 'amelioration', a British euphemism for special category conditions being granted to prisoners (that is *politicals*) arrested under the Defence of the Realm Act (DORA) regulations. Among the younger prisoners who took part in the Mountjoy hunger strike, which secured the release of all the prisoners being held under DORA, were teenagers Todd Andrews and the future artist, Cecil Ffrench Salkeld. Andrews would be in prison on two further occasions while Salkeld's links with Mountjoy would be renewed a generation later when his daughter Beatrice married Brendan Behan—after he himself had spent several years in an English borstal, in Mountjoy and the Curragh.

In typical British fashion, however, an attempt was made to deprive some of those 'entitled' to this hard-won special status by adding a clause stipulating the length of sentence required to qualify. This led, during Christmas week 1918, to a major riot and siege in Crumlin Road Jail when attempts were made to remove a short-term prisoner named John Doran from the republican wing. The ensuing battle lasted three days and saw the virtual destruction of A Wing with dividing walls between cells being breached, the roof destroyed and balconies and stairs in the wing ripped from their moorings. The British brought in a Lewis gun and threatened to kill everyone if Doran was not surrendered. Doran did not surrender and the prisoners won their battle, but many were eventually deported to English jails.

GERMAN PLOTS AND INSECTS

By 1918 as plans for armed struggle were underway, round-ups occurred and the population of the prisons grew steadily as did the number of deportations. An attempt at introducing conscription in Ireland was met with organised and almost total opposition and a 'government' of the nationalist and republican leadership was convened to oppose it. Over seventy leaders from the incipient Republican Movement (almost all of them political rather than military), and others from the broader labour and nationalist movement, were arrested in early 1918. The British made wild and unsubstantiated allegations of their involvement in a 'German Plot', in the final months of World War One. Those arrested were deported to prisons in England.

Prisoners were held in Lincoln Prison, and had what amounted to political status. Conditions were reasonably good. Women internees, including Madame Markievicz, Madame Mac Bride and Kathleen Clarke, were held in Holloway Prison. Their different backgrounds proved a source of entertainment for Kathleen, who was, to say the least, impatient with the genteel demands and unsolicited attentiveness of her two companions, and their constant 'one-up-womanship' as the two tried to compete for who had the highest social standing. She was blatantly insulted when Marchievicz wondered, 'Why on earth did they arrest such a quiet, insignificant person as you?' Kathleen bluntly told her to 'ask the British government' and sarcastically told her that what was on her charge sheet was the same as what was on all their charge sheets![78]

It was from Lincoln that Eamonn de Valera, Sean McGarry and Sean Milroy escaped in February 1919, using a key modelled on life-sized images drawn on a Christmas card sent from the prison six weeks earlier. Sean Milroy was a prolific artist during his ten months' internment. Milroy drew accurate scale cartoons of the key and keyhole

[78]   Clarke, Kathleen (1991) *Revolutionary Woman*. Dublin: The O'Brien Press.

for the Christmas cards which were sent back surreptitiously through the censor, to Ireland. These images allowed IRA engineers to prepare blank keys which would facilitate de Valera's escape, with Sean McGarry and Milroy. The initial smuggled keys didn't work but a prisoner named Peter de Loughrey, a locksmith from Kilkenny, managed to create a master key from a smuggled 'blank' and an impression taken from the prison chaplain's set of keys using wax from a candle by the prison altar boy, Eamon de Valera, during mass.

The Insect

Milroy also made a set of drawings satirically depicting his prison comrades as 'The Insects of Lincoln'.[79] The prison newspaper circulating among prisoners in Lincoln at the time was known as *The Insect*, copies of which Sean O'Mahony kept safe through his prison days.

The Insect was a handwritten bi–monthly journal which ran to three issues beginning on 1 September 1918, and which contained the usual mixture of prison humour, satire, some poetry, and some articles in Irish. Terence McSwiney (one of six prisoners in Lincoln Prison elected in the 1918 General Election[80]) wrote in Irish for *The Insect* while the journal also contained poems by Sean McGarry in the 1 September 1918 edition, and another by Eamon de Valera ('To My Mollie') in the 20 October 1918 issue.[81] It is interesting that Terence McSwiney wrote for this prison paper in Irish for Blythe mentions in his memoirs that McSwiney had never written in Irish for any of Griffiths' Reading Jail publications.

The first tongue in cheek editorial of *The Insect* gave an indication of its political mission when it stated that 'the paper would devote its columns to one cause alone: the time honoured and unconquered cause of *Insectarianism*', a philosophy which the editor defined as 'raising insects from the dark places they have been forced to inhabit and secure for them a place in the sun', and to 'voice their singular & unique merits, to vindicate their claims and to demand that in the hour when all the wild beasts in the Jungle of civilization are clamouring for self determination the modest claims of the lowly insects to determine their own fate and destiny shall not be lightly dismissed.'[82] It was supreme irony.

79 https://westmeathculture.ie/decade-of-centenary/with-the-insects-at-lincoln/
80 Declan Dunne lists the prisoners as Colivet, de Valera, Etchinham, McCabe, McSwiney, O'Mahony. Dunne, Declan (2012) *Peter's Key*. Cork: Mercier Press (P.114).
81 https://catalogue.nli.ie/Record/MS_UR_001692.
82 *The Insect* (1918) Vol 1, No, 1, September 1918 NLI: MS. 24,458.

The Insect had a poetry competition which attracted entries from most of the wing. Poems were to be written with the title 'My Girl', a title of its time and era. *The Insect* articles included two humorous 'election manifestos' from Peadar de Loughrey, and from Séamus Dobbyn for the position of quartermaster of the wing. De Loughrey wrote of his skills as a quartermaster during a previous period in the role and of his unending supply of handballs, and of the joy his election would bring to Rome (a city he had once visited and his stories of which he regularly regaled the wing with). He advised his voters, 'never trust a man with a beard ... especially a Belfastman with a beard!'

Dobbyn, on the other hand, recalled for the electorate the shortage of matches which had fallen on the wing during the previous quartermaster's term of office, assuring the electorate that he had resolved this during a previous spell as QM, creating a reliable lighting system. Satirically, or perhaps in a mild dog whistle, he also warned of 'a perceptible weakening of the moral tone of our community' since his last spell in office, with 'those sewers of iniquity, the English Sunday papers, which I banished from our midst as St Patrick banished the snakes, began to creep in. And this I allege to be solely due to the reprehensible moral depravity of my successor.' With these two issues in mind, he appealed to the electorate on the grounds of 'light and morality' to stand against 'darkness and depravity'.[83]

The paper also scoffed at the 'German Plot' and contained articles and cartoons parodying the erudite and scholarly de Valera; election addresses to voters in a Fermanagh by-election, and to the Cumann na mBan in Galway for another by-election; poems and songs and political analysis.

The remaining 'German Plot' internees were released in May 1919, many months after the surrender of the German Government with whom they had been allegedly conspiring. The prisoners were released to an Ireland which was now at war with Britain, and which had its own (albeit, outlawed) parliament. Arrests and releases under The Cat and Mouse Act continued unabated.

By the following year, in the summer of 1920, the British Government had concluded that the powers of DORA (the Defence of the Realm Act), a war-time measure, were not extensive enough for the purpose they had in mind of suppressing the Irish freedom struggle. The Act had been amended and tampered with since 1914, and they now decided to replace DORA with the Restoration of Order in Ireland Act

---

83   *The Insect* (1918) manifestos. NLI: MS. 24,458.

1920. This new act would allow, for example, for the internment of prisoners on Irish soil, where the powers of DORA had required their internment in British camps like Frongoch or Lincoln or Reading prisons. The first of several Irish internment camps was quickly constructed in Ballykinlar, in County Down, and opened for its initial round-up of prisoners in November 1920.

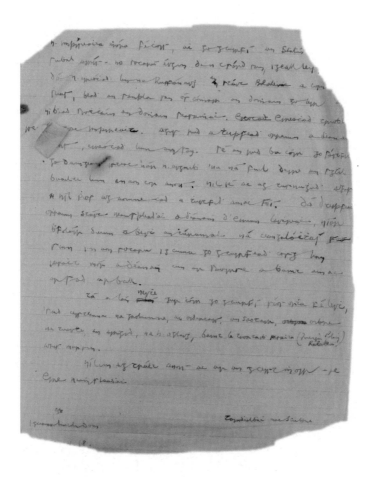

Toirbhealach Mac Suibhne (Terence MacSwiney) writing in *The Insect*. National Library of Ireland

BALLYKINLAR

Among those to arrive there during the opening few weeks was the Maghera solicitor, Louis J Walsh, who was among a group of internees transferred from Derry Jail where he had been detained pending internment. While in Derry Jail, Walsh had begun 'to write some doggerel about the life and humours of the prison that passed from cell to cell'.[84] His manuscripts were untitled and perhaps were not true 'newspapers' but his scribblings went from person to person and the verses were a record of prison life. Walsh was a writer whose dramatic works had once been performed by a British Army dramatic group in Ballykinlar—composed and performed prior to his arrest. Now they were once again performed in Ballykinlar but ironically this time performed among the internees.

Walsh was released in 1921 and his musings were recorded in his prison memoir *On My Keeping and in Theirs,* which was published immediately after his release while prisoners were still being held in Ballykinlar. The book was not, however, widely welcomed in the camp. Proinsias Ó Dubhthaigh, OC of the prisoners in Ballykinlar, expressly told the Bureau of Military History in his submission to the Bureau thirty years later that he had ordered the public burning of Walsh's book at a general parade of POWs in Ballykinlar in protest at the ex-POW revealing secrets from the life of the camp! It was certainly an extreme form of what we might today call 'cancel culture'.

Ballykinlar was a huge prison camp. Not since the days of Frongoch in 1916 had so many republican prisoners been caged together in one prison. It was, in fact, two prisons since Ballykinlar, like Frongoch, consisted of camps numbered I and II, which were in very close physical proximity but separated by British soldiers stationed in overlooking sentry posts. There was little or no movement permitted

---

84   Walsh, Louis J (1921) *On My Keeping and in Theirs.* Dublin: The Talbot Press (P.29).

between Camp I and Camp II during the fourteen months of its existence apart from visits to the shared prison hospital. So strictly was this rule of no contact imposed that three internees were murdered for allegedly coming too close to the boundary wire.

Joseph Tormey and Patrick Sloane were shot dead on 17 January 1921, killed by a single round that passed through Tormey and then struck Sloane killing them instantly. On 15 November 1921 another tragedy occurred when Tadhg Barry was murdered by a sentry as he stood near the fence waving farewell to some comrades from his native Cork who were being released. The Truce was four months in place by this stage, the Treaty only three weeks away.[85] No British soldier was ever held to account for the murders.

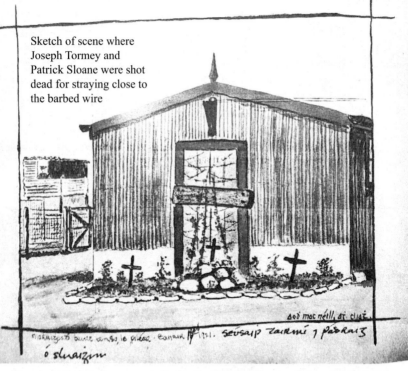

Sketch of scene where Joseph Tormey and Patrick Sloane were shot dead for straying close to the barbed wire

---

85   A number of prisoners were shot dead within the prisons over the years, including Patrick White, shot dead in 1921 during a hurling match on Spike Island when retrieving a sliotar that had gone to the boundary wire. Peadar Breslin was shot dead by Free State soldiers in A Wing, Mountjoy Prison in October 1922. In December 1940 Military Police shot Bernard Casey dead in cold blood while he was queuing for his breakfast (four other prisoners were wounded the same day). Hugh Coney was shot by British soldiers in Long Kesh in November 1974, while Tom Smith was shot dead in Portlaoise Prison on St Patrick's Day, 1975.

Ná Bac Leis, The Barbed Wire

Life in the camps was very well organised and there were numerous military lectures, sporting events, handicrafts, and educational classes. The camps boasted a Dramatic Society and an orchestra. The two camps both had well-stocked libraries and, of course, camp newspapers. There were two different papers in production in Ballykinlar in 1921. In Camp I the paper was called *Ná Bac Leis*, while in Camp II the paper was called *The Barbed Wire*. In some ways the different standards of production reveal the distinct nature of the two camps which came tantalisingly close along one perimeter, divided by a few metres of roadway, and yet the organisational structure from one to the other developed quite differently. Camp I, for example, had its own currency printed, cardboard 'coins' professionally printed in Dublin and whose worth was strictly controlled to match the total 'economy' held in each prisoner's personal prison account. (Paper 'chits' had previously been in use until it was discovered that there were more chits in circulation than what was actually held in the camp coffers). Camp II's paper was always a hand-written, copied manuscript which was labour intensive, while Camp I circulated multiple copies of *Ná Bac Leis*, printed (or *stylographed*) on an early Roneo duplicator each month.

Internees and huts, Ballykinlar, 1921

The ability to produce a 'printed' paper within the camp gives some indication of the freedom or control over their daily routines the prisoners had achieved behind the wire. Art O'Donnell, Commandant of the West Clare Brigade, had been imprisoned on several occasions between 1916 and 1920, being a participant in protests which included the wrecking of Mountjoy Jail and Crumlin Road Prison, hunger strikes in Cork and Mountjoy, work strikes and generally making the prisons unworkable. He considered every action taken against the prison regime as part of the ongoing fight by tying up the British military in guard duties and thus depleting the British forces available to wage war against the IRA.

O'Donnell was part of the group behind the paper *Ná Bac Leis* produced in Camp 1. It is possible that the name *Ná Bac Leis* was recycled from an earlier republican newssheet. Liam de Róiste wrote in his diary on 5 June 1915: 'Sinn Féin and other papers have been suppressed, there is again no lack of patriotic literature. There are *Tracts for the Times* published by Óglaigh headquarters; *The Volunteer*, run by Eoin MacNeill; *The Catholic Bulletin*; the halfpenny *Spark*, (openly seditious). *The Leader* while not Sinn Féin, is not pro-British. There is a little Sheet called *Ná bac leis*. And, I learn today that James Connolly has a new workers' paper going: *The Workers' Republic*.'[86] The re-deployment of names was a common occurrence.

Years later Art O'Donnell recalled the production of *Ná Bac Leis*: 'We needed a typewriter and duplicator to circulate our paper. Through a friend in Dublin, I was able to get a portable Corona Typewriter and a second-hand Roneo Duplicator, with a supply of stencils and duplicating paper.'

The items were boxed-up in a wooden tea-chest and dispatched to the prison camp but by the time the equipment arrived a protest was in progress and all parcels were being stopped or held over. Ironically, this delay in distributing prisoners' parcels may well have worked to the advantage of the internees because when the protest ended a backlog of items belonging to prisoners needed cleared.

'When the strike was finished, all the parcels were taken in and were being examined in the Parcels Office,' recalled Art O'Donnell. 'Among them was a tea-chest which contained the typewriter, duplicator, paper and a bottle labelled "lubricating oil". The censor, intrigued by the

86 Liam Roche (de Roiste): https://www.militaryarchives.ie/collections/online-collections/bureau-of-military-history-1913-1921/reels/bmh/BMH.WS1698%20PART%201.pdf (P.194).

appearance of the oil, decided to smell it and found that it smelled like whiskey, so he ordered the whole box to be put aside for confiscation, and continued his work, giving an occasional glance at the box. However, other people wanted that box too, and before the censor, Captain Farrer, realised what was happening the whole box had disappeared.'[87]

No trace of the missing box, printer or 'oil' was found in the course of a hasty search which followed as soon as Farrer realised that it was missing, but the British captain would eventually learn—on the last night before the prisoners were released—what had become of the lubricating oil. O'Donnell told him that 'the boys drank it'.

Ná Bac Leis appeared regularly, and O'Donnell recalled that many excellent contributors helped ensure that the five- or six-page paper was produced. Joseph Senan Considine acted as editor and Hugo Mac Neill as caricaturist for the paper. Considine was also a prolific poet and wrote of his experiences in Ballykinlar and later as a republican prisoner during the Civil War in Hare Park and in Mountjoy Prison.[88] Around fifty copies of each issue were sold with profits going to the camp funds.

The weekly, hand-transcribed copies of *The Barbed Wire* tended to be shorter while the monthly and larger *Ná Bac Leis* could afford the

---

87   Art O'Donnell: https://www.militaryarchives.ie/collections/online-collections/bureau-of-military-history-1913-1921/reels/bmh/BMH.WS1322.pdf (P.66).

88   Joseph S Considine: 'Poems of Prison Camp and Cells', NLI: MS 34,956 A.

space for articles discussing, for example, the current clothing fashion in Ballykinlar ('The Psychology of Modern Dress in Ballykinlar' by MJ Tierney), or poetry and prose and, occasionally, Irish language articles. Both papers contained humour with snippets of the '*we hear* ...' variety, recording anecdotes (true or exaggerated) from around the camps. Both also followed the tradition of editorial replies to fictitious letter writers and sport, while drama and concerts in the camp were all covered and reviewed.

Politics and culture were also discussed in the papers, as was the prisoners' link with the outside struggle. In *The Barbed Wire* in August 1921, for example, support was expressed for a campaign to support native produce, something advocated by Conradh na Gaeilge/The Gaelic League, while a notice of thanks regarding books for the prison library gives a useful historic footnote as it shows the level of support the prisoners had from what was becoming a society which had begun acting separately from the despised British rule in Ireland. Among contributors to the 2,000 book library, which had been assembled in a matter of months, were the Christian Brothers' School in Synge Street; University College Cork; The Society of Friends in Dublin; The Talbot Press in Dublin; and many individuals.'[89] The paper also notes, tongue in cheek, that only Irish labour and paper was used in producing the journal.[90] Both papers contained their fair share of verse, good and bad, since, as Joseph Campbell remarked a few years later in his Curragh Camp diary, 'Poetry, like scabies, always breaks out in jail.'

89   *The Barbed Wire (1921)*: Issue: August 1921, (P.6) Courtesy Róisín Nic Liam, Corcaigh).
90   *The Barbed Wire (1921)*: Issue: August 1921, (P.6) Courtesy Róisín Nic Liam, Corcaigh).

SPIKE ISLAND

Saoirse

The Spike Island journal *Saoirse* made its one and only appearance on the 9 October 1921, with an opening editorial in Irish. 'Sé Mac Uí Frizelle an Eagarthóir,' it announced.[91] He then invites anyone with ideas to contact the editor, and not to let shyness or lack of confidence put anyone off from writing to the paper. Mac Uí Frizelle was Nicholas J Frizelle, one of the oldest men in the camp at fifty-five-years of age, interned in Spike Island since August 1921.[92] The editorial mentioned that, 'Tá a fhios agaibh gur deineadh iarracht páipéar mar seo a chur ar bun agus b'éigean don eagarthóir imeacht go Béara sula raibh uain aon ní a dhéanamh.' ('You know that an attempt was made to start a paper like this but that the editor was moved to Bere [Island— another internment camp] before anything was done.')

It was autumn 1921, the Truce had been in place for three months, negotiations were taking place and the Treaty was only two months away. Prisoners were, naturally, uneasy and the paper wanted to combat lethargy and prepare prisoners for a resumption of the struggle if need be. The editorial encouraged the prisoners not to be idle:

Ní raibh aon coinne ag éinne again go mbeimis anseo ar theacht an gheimhridh. Anseo atáimid, áfach, cé go bhfuilimid bréan de agus is baolach go mbeimid anseo go ceann tamaill maith eile. Má bhriseann an Fhógra Shíochána, ní bheimid inár gcumas cabhrú le hArm na hÉireann ar pháirc an áir is ní bheidh súil acu le cabhair uainne. Cé nach mbeidh sé de ráth orainn seasamh leo-san nílimid ag rá gur cheart duinn bheith scartha díomhuain anseo.[93]

91   *Saoirse* (1921) Issue 1, 9ú Deireadh Fómhair 1921 (P.4) NLI Holdings: MS 10,913.
92   O'Neill, Tom (2021) *Spike Island's Republican Prisoners, 1921* Cheltenham: The History Press (P.213).
93   *Saoirse* (1921) Issue 1, 9ú Deireadh Fómhair 1921 (P.2) NLI Holdings: MS 10,913.

(No-one expected to be here by the winter but here we are, and while we might be fed-up with it, there's a chance we could be here for a long while to come. If the Ceasefire collapses, we aren't in a position to assist the Army of Ireland on the battlefield nor are they expecting help from us, but while we aren't lucky enough to be standing with them we should not be idle here.)

The editorial went on to say that prisoners had a chance, for example, to learn the language and that they were happy to see that many had started on that task already. The successful propagation of the Irish language was, of course, an important aspiration for the Republican Movement. Many had arrived at *republicanism* through the work of Conradh na Gaeilge and, in turn, many republicans had taken up the work of Conradh na Gaeilge to complete their ideological motivations. But the reality was that the number of Irish language writers was not as great as the editor would have wished: 'It is to our shame that a portion of this paper must appear in a foreign language,'[94] he wrote, and, indeed, apart from the editorial the paper was all in English.

In October 1921 the paper recorded that Spike Island held 552 prisoners: 361 of these were held in A Block, and 191 in B Block.[95] The journal catered for a variety of interests in its pages, with hurling advice (telling prisoners who did not have the skills to learn from their comrades who did) and talking about a proposed hurling match at some future date between a team of the Spike Island and Bere Camp internees playing against a combined Ballykinlar and Hare Park team.

The poetry section was much more spiritual and religious than poetry found in other prison journals, probably reflecting the overall tone of the paper which had for its motto: 'God, our country and the welfare of our comrades'; while political and military articles included a reflection by an anonymous author who recalled a chance meeting with Roger Casement after his arrest. Another article, again written anonymously, was about a Gaelic League organiser at the turn of the century meeting a young schoolboy while travelling as a *Timire* (organiser) and teaching in local schools. Then, twenty years later, still working as a *Timire*, and meeting the same boy, now as a young man and leader of a Flying Column. The author writes of his honour of being present during an attack on a convoy of Black and Tans. There was no

---

94   *Saoirse (1921)* Issue 1, 9ú Deireadh Fómhair 1921 (P.7) NLI Holdings: MS 10,913.
95   *Saoirse (1921)* Issue 1, 9ú Deireadh Fómhair 1921 (P.54) NLI Holdings: MS 10,913.

doubting the linkage of cultural and national struggle.

Saoirse also contained an article examining the possibilities facing 'Labour in the New Irish State'; a satirical 'Open letter to Lloyd George'; and a couple of more reflective articles looking at 'The resurrection of the national spirit' between 1916 and 1921. An allegorical 'Landscape Garden' essay recalled the clearing of the Irish people from their own lands.

The internees of Spike Island were moved, some to Kilkenny Jail and the rest to Maryborough (Portlaoise) Prison in mid-November 1921, and the camp was no longer employed as a prison by the British. No second edition of the journal *Saoirse* was ever produced.

CIVIL WAR EDITIONS

By every metric the brutal response of the Free State against former republican comrades who opposed the Treaty went beyond anything that had ever been inflicted by the British. There were more executions, more assassinations and extra-legal murders, more imprisonment by a factor of four or five of both men and women, more deaths in prison, by bullet or on hunger strike, and more prison brutality, censorship and deprivation than anything conceived by John Bull.

From June 1922 until late in 1924 (and for some unfortunate internees, as late as 1925 and 1926) thousands of prisoners were held, with some estimates putting the number interned at 13,000, of which between six and seven hundred were women. Mountjoy Jail was the first and last port of call for some prisoners. Rifle fire and revolver shots were the soundtrack of the prison and left the newly-established state with a record of sheer infamy in the eyes of many of its citizens.

The first prisoner of the Civil War was said to be Tom Barry, who was arrested while trying to enter the Four Courts and taken straight to Mountjoy, although Leo Henderson, arrested on 26 June 1922 may in fact hold that distinction. Leo Henderson was arrested by Free State troops after he was involved in seizing a number of cars from Ferguson's Garage in Dublin to prevent them being sold in the North, in breach of an IRA boycott of northern unionist businesses. In reprisal for Henderson's arrest the Four Courts HQ arrested a Free State officer, Ginger O'Connell, and from that the situation rapidly deteriorated and the Civil War began with a full scale attack by Free Staters on the Four Courts.

With the fall of the Four Courts and the end of the battle in Dublin hundreds of volunteers were taken prisoner and locked in a prison now being run by former comrades like Phil Cosgrove and Pádraig Ó Caoimh (or as he was better known, Paudeen O'Keeffe). O'Keeffe was

Kilmainham Gaol Museum and National Library of Ireland

nominally the deputy governor but in reality he was the power behind the throne in the day-to-day running of the prison. Cosgrove, a 1916 combatant who had been sentenced to death and later reprieved, was not in good health in 1922. He was, by now, a chronic alcoholic and was appointed prison governor on the coat-tails of his more ruthless brother, WT Cosgrove. Under Cosgrove's short reign as governor there were riots, escapes and executions. He held his former comrades—with whom he had been interned in Ballykinlar—in the most brutal of prison conditions.

However, he was also credited with preventing Free State soldiers from running amok and shooting prisoners at the time of an attempted escape.

Of the many memoirs of the period, only Margaret Buckley, Peadar O'Donnell or Ernie O'Malley, offer any words in recognition of a few small acts of decency by Cosgrove. Cosgrove smuggled out of the prison a couple of letters from the badly-injured O'Malley, at a time when all republicans were to be held incommunicado.[96] O'Malley himself was waiting to be courtmartialled and, in all likelihood, sentenced to death. Only a doctor's refusal to declare O'Malley 'fit enough to die' kept him alive long enough until the Civil War and the executions ended.

Other prisoners held Cosgrove in disdain. Joseph Campbell who had spent a bleak time in Mountjoy in 1922 showed no sympathy at hearing the news of his former governor's death in October 1923: 'Phil Cosgrave dead. I talked loudly about Mountjoy and the execution of Rory O'Connor etc. I hope he'll get more justice in the next world that he gave us in the Joy. Couldn't have better luck. Well Sunday, dead Monday.'[97]

It was a time of little concern over the misfortune of one's enemies.

Between 1922–24 several manuscript newspapers appeared at various times in Mountjoy Prison, with titles such as *The Book of Cells*; *The Sniper*; *The Trumpeter* (*When Gabriel Blows the Last Rally*); *An Barr Buaidh*; and *C-Weeds*.

The Book of Cells

This journal was produced in C Wing and was edited by Liam Mellows. Between June and December 1922 Mellows and Peadar O'Donnell grew very close in the prison, trying to develop a sense of history of the struggle. Mellows wrote: '[N]aturally, we are thinking hard here, though the place and atmosphere is not conducive to thought.'[98] From some of the discussions they had together, ideological positions were

96 Despite attempts to isolate and silence them, the republicans had multiple 'lines' in and out of the prison in most of the prisons and camps.

97 Campbell, Joseph (2001) *As I was Among the Captives.* Cork: Cork University (P.94).

98 Mellows, Liam (1922) *Notes from Mountjoy* Dublin: The Freeman's Journal, September 22, 1922.

perfected and theorised. Before the vengeful executions of Mellows and his comrades Joe McKelvey, Rory O'Connor and Dick Barrett he had produced *Notes from Mountjoy* which were published in the *Freeman's Journal* in September 1922.

Perhaps the *Notes* gave the Free Staters all the reasons they needed to murder Mellows with his unapologetic, searing conclusion that the Treatyites were never with the Republic:

> In our efforts now to win back public support to the Republic we are forced to recognise—whether we like it or not—that the commercial interests so-called—money and gombeen-man—are on the side of the Treaty, because the Treaty means Imperialism and England. We are back to Tone—and it is just as well—relying on that great body, 'the men of no property.' The 'stake in the country' people were never with the Republic. They are not with it now—and they will always be against it—until it wins.[99]

It was to *The Book of Cells,* however, that Peadar O'Donnell attributes his first attempts at becoming a writer, and this paper—written in a prison exercise book—was every bit as critical of the Free State as *Notes from Mountjoy.* O'Donnell would later recall: 'I began to write in 'C' Wing. It arose out of an enterprise of Mellow's. He began a journal called *The Book of Cells* and contributed its main story called "Islanditis". At this time the Treatyite government suggested that the principal prisoners should be transported and Mellows made the possibilities of the adventure before us become rather a promise than a threat.'[100]

This threat of the Free Staters colluding with the British and deporting Irish republicans to a British colony (possibly the Seychelles) was a real threat, mentioned in other memoirs of the time by Seán MacBride and by Ernie O'Malley. In the end, the Free Staters simply built more jails as the logistics and optics of deporting republicans to a British colony were considered too daunting, even for the Free State Government.

O'Donnell remembered very little of the content, '… except unimportant details', but he was attached to the publication. '*The Book of Cells* is ducted into my memory of the jails with vivid aliveness.'

---

99   Mellows, Liam (1922) *Notes from Mountjoy* Dublin: The Freeman's Journal, September 22, 1922.
100   O'Donnell, Peadar (2013) *The Gates Flew Open.* Cork: Mercier (P.41).

They attacked with satire their captors and Free State leaders. 'Quite a number of the cell sheets were written but the fever of the war was in them all.'[101] Mellows would write about Eoin Mac Neill, and O'Donnell would retort with a description of Desmond Fitzgerald: 'He wore a faded cockney accent that he had rinsed in Oxford on the way to Rathmines,'[102] or a similar lambast against Ernest Blythe, both now Free State ministers. In these satirical attacks there was a derision of the perceived snobbery of Blythe and Fitzgerald, the latter of whom was also derided in Todd Andrews' memoir as being 'Librarian in Tintown' during internment by the British in 1921 and holding forth in conversation with only those he felt as intellectual equals; or as Andrews depicted him, 'the most important man in the camp'.

Eventually, O'Donnell would 'become aware of life outside the range of the fever' and so began creative literature, writing the opening scene of his later work *Storm*. However, the new writing vocation was short-lived: 'The creative career was to be disrupted when the magic word "escape" rocketed into my mind and I shot up to it as never fish flashed for a fly'.[103] The escape attempt failed and tragically one prisoner, Peadar Breslin, was shot dead. O'Donnell would soon be shifted and shunted from jail to jail as the Civil War continued, always with the threat of execution hanging over him. A year later, and with a ceasefire in place, he was imprisoned in Finner Camp. He demanded that his personal property be returned to him: his books and his copy of *The Book of Cells*. But, alas, he never got it back.[104]

The Book of Cells was like many other jail newspapers and journals. The opening editorial stated unapologetically that it was 'the duty of every republican prisoner to keep up morale and to prevent their principles and their faith being sapped by jail surroundings' and that 'it is with the idea of stimulating thought and preventing mental apathy that the *The Book of Cells* is presented to the cellmates of Mountjoy.'

The editors wrote that 'if they have succeeded in helping one prisoner to while away a dreary hour and caused even one prisoner to renew his dreary spirit, in common with the contributors, the artists and the publishing staff will feel repaid a hundredfold.'[105]

---

101 O'Donnell, Peadar (2013) *The Gates Flew Open*. Cork: Mercier (P.42).

102 O'Donnell, Peadar (2013) *The Gates Flew Open*. Cork: Mercier (P.42).

103 O'Donnell, Peadar (2013) *The Gates Flew Open*. Cork: Mercier (P.42).

104 O'Donnell, Peadar (2013) *The Gates Flew Open*. Cork: Mercier (P.136).

105 *The Book of Cells* (1922) NLI MS 20849 (P.3) The copy in the National Library is a lengthy but partial transcript of some articles from *The Book of Cells* but does not have the artwork mentioned.

One article, 'Up the Republic', was clearly designed to encourage men whose faith in the ability of republican forces matching the fury and resources of the Free State was on the wane. While their jail conditions were truly appalling, the editorial piece argued that despite their imprisonment the *Republic* remained alive, with the appointment of a President and a Council of State.

Maltreatment was also the focus of the longest chapter of *The Book of Cells*, the caustic, satirical piece imagined by Mellows and O'Donnell of a cabinet meeting of the Free State Government to discuss the transportation of republican prisoners to some remote island at the behest of, and with the support of, the British Government.[106] Their Free State enemies were depicted in the worst possible light as military peacocks, buffoons and drunkards, arriving late for the cabinet meeting and under the influence of drink. The President of the Cabinet, WT Cosgrave, described as 'a chucker-outer becoming a chucker-inner' and 'a grocer's curate', whose only previous experience of decision making was in the minor role of a Rural District Councillor. O'Higgins, Blythe, Mulcahy, and the rest were all lampooned. The paper can be dated between August and December of that tragic year, since the cabinet 'meeting' makes no mention of Michael Collins or Arthur Griffiths, both of whom died in August 1922, while Mellows was vindictively executed on 8 December in Mountjoy.

The Trumpeter, The Sniper

Another Mountjoy compilation, was a twenty-four-page handwritten paper, the pages written front and back with some colours on the cover and on certain headline pages inside. It was a monthly journal, in circulation in A Wing in November and December 1922. Issue No.1 appeared in November 1922 and carried a fairly barbed 'Welcome' to a new contemporary paper also being published in A Wing, *The Sniper*. It was an odd welcome, considering that the first issue of *The Sniper* was in circulation a few days before *The Trumpeter*, but unusual as it may seem the two papers appeared as rivals. *The Sniper* opened with an editorial placing the paper and prison struggle in the tradition of O'Donovan Rossa and Clarke. These lofty thoughts were dismissed by *The Trumpeter*'s editorial which proclaimed:

---

106   Fact is stranger than fiction. The correspondence to the plan was revealed in a Michael Portillo documentary on the Civil War on the BBC in May 2023.

The motives and sentiments embodied in the first article of *The Sniper* and coupled with the names of two great men of our race … are commendable to all but our position today differs somewhat from theirs. We should not be content to remain listlessly within prison bars … (we) should not be silent and inactive participators in the glorious struggle of the men outside. Platitudes serve no good purpose. They are not an incentive to any good cause; they are but the vapourings of weaklings. To talk about what our grandfathers did will not get us anywhere.'

Another *Trumpeter* article continued in this vein by condemning the satirical pieces in *The Sniper* 'in having recourse to this crude method of making *jokes* at others expense'. *The Sniper* was being edited by Art O'Connor and Joseph Campbell. Curiously, Campbell makes no reference to the paper in his diaries, nor of the dispute between the papers. In the paper's editorial which raised the ire of *The Trumpeter*, O'Connor had written that 'they intend to keep everyone in the wing awake, and rouse those who may be growing weary, to stimulate those who are faint, to encourage those who are manfully plodding along'.

Campbell's article on chivalry attacked 'the Green Knights of Cosgrave's Cabinet' who were violating 'a most treasured national virtue' of chivalry to women. While it may appear paternalistic the article in fact listed women who had been active since 1916—Mary McSwiney, Madame O'Rahilly, Shiela Humphries etcetera—and the treatment being meted out to them by the Free State. Campbell's article however gave the rivals in *The Trumpeter* another rod to beat them with, as the following paragraph showed:

Apropos to J Campbell's reminder that there is such as thing as Irish chivalry—it would be well if a little was exercised in this wing. While Mary MacSwiney's body and mind are being racked by the agonies of a hunger strike, yahoos choose the time for assinine yelling and cheering. When chivalry demands silence our 'Knights' consider Scully's[107] antics or Jerry Irwin's speed exhibits in the ring as fit objects to call for vociferous cheering. Call a halt.

107   Scully, a stray cat which had made its home in the wing.

An analytical contribution on 'The Situation in Politics' by Robert Barton, which examined the lack of legitimacy of the Free State, was criticised in equally dismissive terms in *The Trumpeter* where a contributor felt his analysis was 'clear as mud' and 'it does not require realms of argument to justify our position. We are soldiers sworn to maintain the Republic and we will maintain it.' It was clearly a time of comrades watching for any signs of weakness or wavering. The tone in many of *The Trumpeter* contributions was aggressive and unflinching. Men who had 'signed the form' were 'weaklings' who 'have gone under the banner of infidelity and apostasy' and were warned 'not to seek to seduce others from their allegiance to the Republic.' Equally unremitting was the full page Special Notice:

> We reserve this page specially to draw attention to the continuous use of filthy obscene expressions—foreign importations from that cesspool of corruption and iniquity—England. Those who are addicted to that practice in this Wing should drop it. Anybody disregarding this order will be publicly pilloried, or perhaps 'get a crooked way of eating his bit'.

Apart from a poem in Irish called 'Éire', there was also an article in Irish in *The Sniper*, 'Gan Teanga, Gan Tír,' which echoed a frequent criticism of the movement—usually raised in a reflective period after imprisonment—that those fighting for political freedom must also engage in the struggle for cultural freedom. On that, at least, the two rival papers could agree and indeed *The Trumpeter* took offence at 'the selfish sot', the 'brainless individual', the 'sneering shoneen', who had scoffed at *The Sniper* article. Strong words, as always.

The paper had, however, its lighter side. Despite criticising *The Sniper* for its 'jokes', *The Trumpeter* carried a satirical short story, satirical poetry, some humourous 'advertisements', and a list of wing 'does and don'ts' or 'Things to be remembered'. This included the warning not to cadge cigarettes from Free Staters.

Issue No. 2 was published on 3 December. The artist who created the cover of the journal, a representation of a bugler standing at the top of the stairs leading to the third-floor landing of A Wing, was C. Boylan who also illustrated the inside of the publication. In Issue No. 1 he had gone by the penname, 'Buck-shee', a widely used word in the prison at the time which often meant something (tobacco, for example) gained for free or illicitly.

Issue No. 2 carried an obituary by Proinnsias Ó Gallachóir on Erskine Childers who had been executed by the Free State in a shocking act of spite on 23 November. Ó Gallachóir (Frank Gallagher), a close friend of Childers, had been in the Republican Publicity Department. He had been on a hunger strike in 1918 (with the diary of that strike recorded in his book *Days of Fear*); and would be part of the final group on hunger strike in 1923. His wife Cecilia (Saunders) spent the Civil War interned in various prisons, sometimes just a hundred yards from her husband, but was never allowed any contact. Cecilia kept a diary of her imprisonment which provides many insights into the lives of her comrades in the womens' prisons.

It was a time of sudden death.

Poems commemorated Cathal Brugha and Harry Boland. Another article titled 'Our Martyrs' opens by remarking that:

> The executions of Erskine Childers and Cassidy, Fisher, Twohig and Gaffney[108] has sent a thrill of indignation and horror through us here ... The late executions, according to Cosgrove, author, President and symbol of all this infamy, perfidy, butchery and tragedy are perpetrated to create a precedent for future executions.[109]

A satirical piece on the prison cat was really a subliminal appeal for better hygiene in the wing. The cat, the author felt, had better hygiene habits than the unidentified culprits in the wing who failed to flush the toilets. The wing cat, was a much-loved symbol of freedom of sorts and was known as Scully. The cat makes cameo appearances in a couple of memoirs of the time, becoming the stuff of legend and lore. One evening after the Free State guards had fired repeated volleys of shots up the wing to force the prisoners to go to their cells the prone figure of a cat was seen outlined in the gloom of the dark wing causing great dismay. The following morning the gloom lifted when it was discovered that it was an another stray cat, and not Scully, who had died for Ireland. The lucky black cat, incidentally, also appears on the graphic masthead of the wing paper *The Sniper*, November 1922.

---

108   Peter Cassidy (21), James Fisher (19), John Gaffney (20) and Richard Twohig (20) were executed together on 17 November 1922. The four unknown and unheralded volunteers, were killed by the Free State because of the very fact that they were unknown, and not famous leaders, in a cruel act designed to facilitate and prepare the public mind for the killing of other, more prominent republicans.

109   *The Trumpeter* (1922) Mounjoy: December 3rd 1922 NLI Ms. 21,121 (P.19).

A more serious article looked at the history of the Fianna, of which there were many members in A Wing in Mountjoy, a point noted, for example, in Joseph Campbell's prison diary. The Fianna lads took particular glee in winding the Deputy Governor of the prison up. Pádraig Ó Caoimh had on a number of occasions, himself been a prisoner and his turn of phrase often made him a caricature of officialdom, boasting for example, that 'nothing escapes from here but gas', when discussing escapes with Andy Cooney, the OC of the Wing. He had been Sinn Féin Secretary in the 1918-21 period and when asked by the Daily Mail during an interview to sum up Sinn Fein policy he defined it as 'Revenge, bejasyus, revenge.' In Mountjoy he was generally considered fair, although Margaret Buckley felt that he couldn't hide his dislike of a large group of Republican women deported from England and lodged in his prison in 1923. In A Wing with the male prisoners and Fianna boys, his night time patrols would be met with wailing taunts of Paud-eeeen while he would stand in the wing, pistols in his hands, demanding to be called by his proper title: *Deputy Governor.*

The Sniper also carried an unsigned, two-page criticism of those failing to take part in the nightly rosary, failing to attend mass, or worst of all, attending mass and using the service as an opportunity to talk and exchange scéal with comrades, was worthy of any encyclical or pastoral letter. This was in a time when priests and chaplains in Mountjoy were refusing the sacraments to prisoners yet expected unquestioning allegiance from the same prisoners in attendance at mass. It was a period best summed up by Peadar O'Donnell's opinion that a historic, traditional Irish blessing that had been in use for hundreds of years among Irish mothers had latterly became a curse in Mountjoy: the greeting of 'May your sons be Bishops' now held all the rage it was possible to muster against both church, and state, when the words were flung at the prison guards by women prisoners between 1922 and 1924.[110]

In *The Trumpeter* the Free State regime was likened to the running of the country by a bar-keeper and drunkards, just as it had been ridiculed in *The Book of Cells*. The sports page is also full of not-so-subtle political double meaning. A half page is devoted to snippets of jail gossip and rumours, while there are two poems from Joseph Campbell, an established writer before and after his imprisonment and

110   It's noteworthy that this particular article contains many Americanisms and phrases like 'side-walk'; 'why Blazes Kate'; or 'nothing doin' Bo'. Perhaps a clue to the author is the one prisoner in Mountjoy who had spent time in the USA and was given to writing, Seán a' Chóta Ó Caomhánach, who was also a close associate of the paper's deputy editor, Joseph Campbell.

whose contemporary diary of the time, *As I Was Among The Captives*, was published almost eighty years later, recalling his time in Mountjoy and in the Curragh Camp.[111] Campbell had, it will be remembered, been associate editor of *The Sniper* a month earlier but that paper seems to have ended after one issue.

Life in Mountjoy was very arbitrary throughout the years 1922-1924 and prisoners were constantly being shifted between wings (and to other prisons). Four of the seventy-seven executions of the Civil War were carried out in the prison and conditions were not always conducive to producing a clandestine paper, regardless of the political motivation and determination, or 'the fever of war' in the minds of the prisoners. It would be the middle of 1923 before the next paper made its debut.

An Barr Buaidh

The National Library of Ireland holds a cover design for *An Barr Buaidh*, sketched by Alfred McLoughlin.[112] That name was also employed as the title of a paper which had been published for some weeks before the 1916 Rising, seven years earlier. Áine Ceannt, prominent republican and Cumann na mBán leader, and widow of the 1916 leader Eamonn Ceannt, recalled that: 'About this period there was in circulation for about six weeks a very advanced paper, written all in Irish and entitled *An Barr Buaidh*. Eamonn Ceannt contributed to nearly every copy of this, and I think Pearse was Editor.'[113] Alfred McLoughlin, incidentally, was a cousin of Pearse.[114]

The cover of his prison journal depicts two Celtic figures ready for battle, while the logo design is of Celtic knotwork with an interwoven dragon. There are no colours in the line drawing which is described in the National Library file as a 'draft' cover, while Kilmainham Gaol Museum has a copy of the first edition of *An Barr Buaidh*, minus a cover. In the introduction to the first issue McLoughlin discusses the name in mythological and heroic language. He declared that: 'The present military and political situation calls for a rallying title that will elevate the minds of our little community to the immortal ideal for

111   Campbell, Joseph (ed. Ní Chuilleanáin, Eiléan) (2001) *As I Was Among The Captives* Cork: Cork University Press.
112   https://catalogue.nli.ie/Record/MS_UR_077336.
113   Ceant, Áine (1949): https://www.militaryarchives.ie/collections/online-collections/bureau-of-military-history-1913-1921/reels/bmh/BMH.WS0264.pdf (P.8).
114   Nugent, Laurence (1953) https://www.militaryarchives.ie/collections/online-collections/bureau-of-military-history-1913-1921/reels/bmh/BMH.WS0907.pdf (P.41).

which we are all thrown here together.' The editors had chosen their name after much consideration: '*An Barr Buaidh*,' he wrote, 'was the wonderful trumpet of warrior Finn with which he was wont to marshall his Fianna to the fray and the resounding blare of which, over hill and vale, froze the blood in the veins and the marrow in the bones of his and Éire's enemies.' Stirring stuff, indeed.

An Barr Buaidh provided a space for prose and poetry, including some verse from the aforementioned Joseph Considine whose prolific pen would produce many republican poems during those years. The paper contained a lengthy Irish language article which argued that with release from prison inevitable at some date, and the military campaign suspended until more opportune times, that now an opportunity— indeed, an obligation—existed to develop an Irish language literature to assist with the language revival. The author of the piece, 'An Duine Doilgheasaigh', declared that he was going to begin translating *Paradise Lost* in weekly installments for the paper as his own contribution to create this new Irish literature. A second, unsigned Irish language article exhorted readers to begin the work again for the language and linked the language struggle with the national struggle:

'Níor dheineadh amhla ins na blianta a d'imigh tharainn. Na fir go raibh baint acu leis an Arm d'fhanadar taobh amuigh den Ghluaiseacht Náisiúnta agus nuair a tháinig an t-am go raibh gnó faoi leith le déanamh bhí sé gan déanamh toisc gan aon tsuim acu siúd ach amháin i gcúrsaí airm … ná déanaimis dearmad d'obair na Gaeilge ach chomh beag mar is í an Teanga bun agus barr an scéil, mar a déarfá. Gan teanga, gan tír.'[115]

Another interesting article, 'Thoughts in Solitary Confinement' was signed by Pádraic Pléamon. Better known perhaps by the English version of his name, Pádraig Fleming, he fought many a lonely battle single-handedly against the prison system and was eminently qualified to write on the subject of solitary confinement. Fleming's solo battles against the prison system merited a full chapter by Loughlin McGlynn in the book *Sworn to be Free: IRA Jailbreaks 1918-1921*.[116] He had been imprisoned by the British in 1917 and spent several weeks being held naked, and on hunger strike demanding political status.

After the death of Tomás Ashe he was released under the Cat and

115 *An Barr Buaidh* (1923) No. 1 'Ag Féachaint Romhainn'. Kilmainham Prison Museum.
116 O'Donoghue, Florence (1971) *Sworn to be Free: The Complete Book of IRA Jailbreaks, 1918-1921*. Dublin: Anvil Books (PP 53-63).

Mouse Act but was re-arrested under the German Plot scam by the British and resumed his protest. This time he was on protest for weeks, each day being forcibly dressed in the prison uniform and manacled to prevent him removing the clothes and held in solitary in conditions akin to those inflicted on O'Donovan Rossa. Eventually he began another hunger strike and again won his freedom.

His article in *An Barr Buaidh* was full of the wise experience he had acquired during his long periods of protest and foreshadowed the 1927 Max Ehrmann poem 'Desiderata' in both style and content: 'Physical courage is a wonderful thing to possess, but it is moral courage will save a nation,' he wrote. 'Practice what you preach,' he said, 'is a good maxim. But even if you fail to live up to this do not hesitate to teach what is good—other may be strong when you are weak.'

C-Weed

The most substantial of the Mountjoy prison papers during the Civil War was *C-Weed*. It survived for at least three issues, the third issue appearing in May 1923. The final issue was contained in a hard-backed exercise book, and supplemented by four pages of cartoons bringing the total paper to almost ninety-eight pages, larger than the previous two papers. This allowed for more thoughtful and in depth articles. One contribution from the paper was reprinted in *The Catholic Bulletin*[117] in September 1923, on the subject of art and the responsibility of Ireland to reclaim her place as a centre of art. It gives a flavour of the paper's contents as a journal containing some reflective writing by prisoners willing to create a new order in the post-British era. The author was Count Plunkett whose son Joseph, a signatory of the Proclamation, had been executed in 1916. The editorial hoped that readers would 'find material both of an amusing and educational character. This is as it should be. Life should not be all pleasure, neither should it be all work, but a blending of both'.[118]

The publication carried the same range of articles as other papers although there was none of the acrimony of *The Trumpeter*. There were poems, mock advertisements and letters, a health column and a mixture of both serious and light, as had been promised. An article, 'What are we doing in Prison', was an appeal to men not to waste the opportunity

---

117 *The Catholic Bulletin* (1923), Vol. XIII, pp. 604-605, September, 1923. NLI Holdings, Call Number:1H 635.
118 *C-Weed* (1923) May 1923, Foreword. Kilmainham Gaol Museum.

which prison gave to study, to learn the language and to keep fit, become propagandist, to understand their enemy. The writer, Tomás Mac Uileagóid (who sometimes wrote under the pen-name, Pro Patria) compared the life of the 200 prisoners in Mountjoy at that time with the education and activities in Hare Park, and also among the women prisoners, saying that they were in 'a hopeless position' but that they needed to organise. In Hare Park, he wrote, there was an education programme:

Monday - Irish (3 classes), English composition, letter writing, French
Tuesday - Shorthand, Agriculture
Wednesday - Elementary book-keeping, Mathematics
Thursday - Drawing, Physics
Friday - English composition, letter writing, French
Saturday - Shorthand, Agriculture

'A time will come when we will look back. We will then ask ourselves what we have done. Many will say 'I learned that in prison'. I studied it first in Mountjoy. Out of C Wing came forth an army of propagandists.'[119]

Tomás Ó Dalaigh penned an article remembering Liam Lynch, killed by the Free State the previous month: 'His grave at Kilcrumper graveyard, where he rests beside his friend and first comrade-in-arms Fitzgerald, shall be visited by Irishmen in future generations seeking inspiration when the names of those arch traitors shall be linked with those of McMurrough and Castlereagh.'

An article signed by Seán Ruiséal (Seán Russell), a future Chief of Staff of the IRA, titled 'Who Has Gone Astray?' challenges the legitimacy of the Free State and in the course of several pages recounts a telling list of how the Free State has been dealing with the families of the 1916 leaders:

Pearse - His mother's house has been raided on several occasions by FS troops
Connolly - His daughter Nora Connolly O'Brien at present under arrest in the S.D. Union

119   *C-Weed* (1923), May 1923, 'What are we doing in Prison?' Kilmainham Gaol Museum.

Clarke - His widow arrested and released and her home raided several times

Ceannt - His widow's home raided and her furniture destroyed

Plunkett - His father at present in this prison. His home raided and property confiscated. His two brothers under arrest in Newbridge and his sister arrested and still in custody.

McDonagh - His brother Joe arrested and died, a prisoner in the hospital attached to this prison.

O'Rahilly - Sister (Mrs Humphries) and niece (Miss S Humphries) both in the custody of the Free State, the latter wounded by FS troops before arrest

McSwiney - Two sisters, Mary and Annie both arrested and released after hunger strike

M Mallon - His son at present in A Wing of this prison undergoing a sentence of five years as a result of his republican activities

Kevin Barry - Two sisters arrested

McBride - His widow and son arrested –the latter still in custody

Dick McKee - His sister a prisoner in the S.D. Union

NDU Invincible

Seán Russell's listing of the way the Free State was arresting and imprisoning mothers and sisters and daughters of the 1916 and Tan War leaders was accurate.

He could have added Grace Gifford to his list as she languished, at that time, in Kilmainham with hundreds of other women. The first group of women prisoners were interned by the Free State in September 1922, with the women initially being held in the hospital wing in Mountjoy Prison. They were later transferred (in a move that was carried out with great brutality) to Kilmainham Gaol, and to The North Dublin Union (NDU), a former workhouse building which neighboured Richmond Prison.

Conditions varied greatly from prison to prison and the women were active in demanding their status as political prisoners; taking part in escapes, protests; suffering violence from male and female guards—

including a Free State womens' corps established to rival Cumann na mBan (which remained loyal to the *Republic*) called Cumann na Saoirse. Pro-Free State women were used for searching and—no pun intended—manhandling female republican prisoners during strip searches or forced moves.

In prison, the women organised themselves with classes and handicrafts and sport, much in the same way as the male prisoners were organised. Mini-festival, sports competitions, concerts, were all arranged while the women also planned and carried out drilling, escapes, and digging tunnels. During a period of hunger strikes, prisoners in the North Dublin Union were joined for a time by Gobnait Ní Bhruadair, (also known as The Hon. Albine Lucy Broderick), a member of the aristocracy who had converted to Irish republicanism post-1916. She had, in fact, managed to gain entry as a visitor to the internment camps in Frongoch six years earlier, one of very few outsiders to have been allowed beyond the prison visiting area. Now, with the Civil War in full motion she was training and active again, and in the Treaty split she had taken the republican side. In the North Dublin Union, she joined other women on hunger strike despite being seriously injured and still recovering from a gunshot wound to her leg sustained during her arrest in Kerry. Broderick was described by Frank Gallagher, writing under his pseudonym David Hogan, as 'that sturdy soul … a stout hearted, indomitable Sinn Féiner.'[120]

In the NDU she was friendly and respected by all the prisoners for her bravery. Hundreds of women from across the social and political milieus of republicanism had been interned as the civil war raged. While the women had a common enemy in the Free State the internal dynamics were at best fractious as differences in class, in allegiance, (to the IRA, to Cumann na mBán, to Sinn Féin, or to family and tradition) and attitudes to prison struggle, led to strained relationships and running disputes between the women.

Among the hundreds of women imprisoned were two sisters: Hannah and Sis Moynihan from Kerry who were being held on charges of publishing a seditious paper named *The Invincible* in their native county. The sisters had been arrested in March 1923 at their home in Tralee and were fascinated to discover when they arrived in Kilmainham that they were being held in a cell that had been occupied by the Invincibles forty years earlier.

120   Hogan, David (1954) *The Four Glorious Years*. Dublin: Irish Press Limited (P.57).

'We are learning something in our wing. The *Invincibles* were imprisoned here, and their graves are in our recreation yards. Parnell's cell is on the ground floor and a dismal one it is too.'[121]

Kilmainham had been lying largely empty and uninhabitable since 1905, apart from a period following Easter Week 1916, until the year 1920. Ernie O'Malley escaped from the prison in February 1921 with Simon Donnelly and Frank Teeling. 1922 saw the arrival of male prisoners again at the beginning of the Civil War followed by the execution of four republican prisoners on 17 November 1922, possibly shot against the same wall as had been used in the execution of the 1916 leaders.

In September 1922 the Free State government began interning women, initially in Mountjoy and then in early 1923, many of them were rough-handedly shifted to the squalor of Kilmainham. The sisters soon decorated their cell with the name The Invincibles, just as other women also gave titles and names to their cells.[122] The women prisoners were being held in A Wing and B Wing of the prison and the sense of separatedness between the wings, and indeed between the different landings on the main wing, were as strong as any parish rivalry outside the prison. A shrine or altar was erected during a hunger strike at one stage on the stairs and women were expected—rostered might be a better description—to attend prayer vigils around the clock. The wings also had memorable nights of entertainment with well-organised Easter commemorations. Direct family members of some of the executed leaders of 1916 were among the prisoners, including Nora Connolly, Grace Plunkett and Maud Gonne MacBride, and this added great poignancy to the event. A pageant on Irish history was organised as part of a late evening inter-wing visit, the women dressing up and making a dramatic processional entrance from the gloom of B Wing into the vast space of A Wing. All agreed that it was a stunning performance.

The tensions, unfortunately, still lingered.

When Hannah and Sis were moved to the North Dublin Union, they arrived in the midst of a protest against overcrowding being staged by the other women who had arrived in the NDU a week earlier. Resentments from Kilmainham were carried on to the NDU. For many

---

121 Moynihan, Hannah (1923), diary entry, 18 March 1923, KMGLM.2010.0246 (P. 29).

122 Many of these cell names remain to this day. Some appear to have been written by prisoners from Derry and Donegal with names such as Carndonagh Hotel, Skeog Patrol and Skeog, Derry Walls, Burnfoot, Dunmore, Foyle and Inch Fort, all carved into the paint above the cell doors.

nights the first group of women to have arrived refused point blank to accept new committals into their wing which, they asserted, was already at capacity. As each new batch of prisoners was moved from Kilmainham Jail to the NDU they were forced to sleep in the yard at night. Arguments festered between the prisoners themselves, as some of the new admissions were less than pleased to be caught up in a protest not of their making.

After some time in the NDU, conditions improved and one day in conversation with Hannah, Gobnait Ní Bhruadair encouraged her to begin a manuscript newspaper. Hannah of course was detained for the offence of creating a mosquito press newspaper, *The Invincible*, and had, since March 1923, been keeping a diary of her prison life. And so she began work on a prison paper of the same name and adding NDU to the title naming it *NDU Invincible*.

The paper was a seven-page, handwritten manuscript. The editorial on the first page explained that the attempt 'to float a chronicle of jail life' was being done at the behest of the Hon A. Broderick and indeed half of the content of the paper had been penned by her too.

A two-page article appealed for unity amongst the women. Pulling no punches, she wrote of, 'difficulties and temptations ... belonging specifically to prison life, petty disputes, petty jealousness, petty growls and grumbles, impatience of the faults of others ...'

Reading the paper, a hundred years later, the repetitive use of 'petty' is very telling. She reminded the readers that: 'We are Republicans, surrounded on every side by an enemy, keen to note every break in our ranks and even the least failure in our unity. To that enemy we must present a united front.'

In a second contribution Ní Bhruadar wrote 'a letter' to the prison governor, comparing him to Brer Rabbit, 'he lie low and say nuffin', accusing him of running scared and hiding at the first sign of trouble while conditions and sanitation in the wing deteriorated. She warned that a day was coming when he would no longer be able to run into his burrow, that the terrier dogs would get him: 'then, only a squeal and— farewell, Brer Rabbit.'

The paper appeared a week after Gobnait's release on 14 May 1924, but within a week the editor was recording in her diary that she had a 'Hot argument with B. Connolly. She made some unfavourable comments on "N.D.U Invincible" and its "vulgarity." How dare she!' [123] wrote Hannah.

---

123   Moynihan, Hannah (1923) diary entry 24 May 1923, KMGLM.2010.0246 (P. 79).

The B. Connolly in question was Bridie Connolly, a veteran of the GPO in 1916, a Cumann na mBán activist throughout the Tan War and part of the Barry's Hotel garrison during the Civil War. Hannah Moynihan's paper may well have fallen short of the standards expected by the Cumann na mBán members in the prison, with its mild satire on 'odoris causa' (bad smells) in the wings, or indeed her parody of her wing comrades (who she branded 'queue cranks') and their 'eagerness to form queues'. However, whether through the rights or wrongs of such sensitivities or the removal of prisoners back to Kilmainham, the NDU Invincible did not survive to Issue 2.

TINTOWN

The largest prison camp of the Civil War was known as Tintown, in the Curragh in Kildare. There were also prisoners held on Spike Island, Athlone, Hare Park, Gormanstown and a dozen other temporary and permanent prisons.

The Tintown Herald

Tintown consisted of three camps: Camps I, II and III. Hare Park was actually within sight of the prisoners in Camp II. Joseph Campbell, writing in his diary in July 1923, refers to a fellow prisoner, Jim Stapleton, as *The Tintown Herald* reporter, but in the style of many of Campbell's diary entries the title may well have been more facetious than factual.[124]

Stapleton is mentioned on a few occasions in the diary as a source of news and rumour. That any copies survive today of any of the camp papers is commendable, considering the awful conditions and never-ending raids and searches to which the republican prisoners were subject. Up to 13,000 men and women were interned, seventy-seven (or eighty-two by some counts) were executed, often with only a matter of hours between verdict and execution, and unofficial assassinations claimed the lives of double that figure.

An entry in a prison autograph book[125] of the period recalls the final message of James O'Rourke, executed on 13 March 1923, in Beggars Bush Barracks. The message was written on his cell wall:

124 Campbell, Joseph (ed. Ní Chuilleanáin, Eiléan) (2001) *As I Was Among The Captives*: Cork University Press (diary reference 30-7-1923).
125 Autograph book belonging to Mícheál Ua Dúnabháin, Mogeely, Co. Cork, compiled in Tintown, courtesy of Danny Morrison.

On a Wall in Mountjoy.

The following was written on wall of cell where James O'Rourke, who was executed in Dublin on March 13th 1923, was confined in Mountjoy :—

"Jas. O'Rourke. 12/3/23.

"Oh my God, the news was startling. I am to be executed at 8 o'clock in the morning. The Angelus is ringing. I never thought I should die for Ireland, but God willed it otherwise. (If I could only see my Mother.) I have 13 hours more to live; every minute brings another life to an end; death is but a release to a troublesome life. Ireland, what a most unfortunate country you are. ?

You have suffered. "

With saddest heart I seep before
Upon my prison bed
But ere I sleep I pray for those
Now lying cold & dead.

April 1923

97

Jas. O'Rourke. 12/3/23

Oh my God, the news was startling. I am to be executed at 8 o'clock in the morning. The Angelus is ringing. I never thought I should die for Ireland, but God willed it otherwise. (If I could only see my mother). I have 13 hours more to live; every minute brings another life to an end; death is but a release from a troublesome life. Ireland, what a most unfortunate country you are. You have suffered.

Four executions took place in Mountjoy, with prisoners also being summarily done to death all across the country, in Kilmainham, Donegal, Galway, Kilkenny, Cork and in the Curragh. It was as if the Free State wanted to 'blood' each province in having a hand in the executions and imprisonment of former comrades, making so many complicit that there was no going back.

Conditions in the camps were grim, although in a strange way the act of being handed an internment order was often welcomed by a prisoner because it probably meant, or was felt to mean, like an escape from the firing squad. Death, and the threat of it, hung over the camps but organisational work continued for most of the period until eventually the uncertainty of their fate led to a collapse of morale. Prisoners were bayoneted and shot on occasions for refusing to comply with the Free Staters orders to dig trenches (to prevent escape attempts). Mass hunger strikes divided rather than united the prisoners. As the Civil War ended in defeat, all combined to weaken men and to lead to demoralisation.

Todd Andrews, interned in the Rath Camp in the Curragh under the British, was re-interned in Newbridge Barracks in 1923 during the Civil War. He painted a very bleak picture of life in the prison. Over 2,500 men were interned there by the time he arrived. He was shocked to find a level of despair where classes were almost non-existent, Irish barely spoken, and disorder was the culture of the camp. The Camp OC, Tom McMahon, and all the Camp Council, had been moved to Mountjoy after an escape attempt:

The prisoners had not got around to choosing a new O/C and the consequent lack of discipline tended to aggravate the general level of discontent that was never far from the surface in any internment camp at that time ...[126]

126   Andrews, CS (2008) *Dublin Made Me*. Dublin: The Lilliput Press (P.316).

I turned my mind to the many contrasts between conditions in Newbridge and life as I remembered it in the Rath Camp under the British regime. In the Rath Camp rugby or soccer would not have been tolerated by the prisoners. The high morale which existed in the Rath had disappeared to be supplanted by the disenchantment of defeat. The future of the nation had no meaning for us. We were waiting more or less stoically to be released. Even release was not looked forward to with much enthusiasm because most of the prisoners had no special future to look forward to. Escape, the great stimulus to the morale of internment camps in any country in any time, was rarely mooted.[127]

Poblacht na hÉireann

Despite Andrews' despairing recall of of his time in Newbridge, a prison paper had been in circulation there in the early part of 1923, before his arrival. The paper's cover page styled it *Poblacht na hÉireann* but the heading on the inside pages gave it the more familiar *An Phoblacht*. The typed pages were in English but the paper included a handwritten page in Irish consisting of lessons and phrases.

Volume 1, No. 5, was published as a 'Sporting Edition' and besides coverage of camp boxing matches, and a report on 'With the Gaels in Newbridge' giving news of camp GAA games and an upcoming fixture of Louth versus Wexford planned for March 1923, the paper carried a round-by-round report of the Siki v McTigue title fight held in Dublin the previous week. That World Light Heavyweight title fight (now considered a major historical marker) was the first international sporting event staged in the new Free State. It was held six days before the publication date of *An Phoblacht* and the report was, in all likelihood, a re-write from another newspaper smuggled into the camp. Other topics covered in *An Phoblacht* included a report of the Ballyseedy Massacre, which had been carried out a fortnight earlier, a review of the drama *Naboclish* performed in the camp and a comment reporting the words of Archbishop Mannix criticising any vote to ratify the treaty: 'A vote now would be that of a terrorised and not a Free Independent people'.[128]

127   Andrews, CS (2008) *Dublin Made Me*. Dublin: The Lilliput Press (P.317).
128   *Poblacht na hÉireann/An Phoblacht* (1923) Vol 1, No 5, 24 March 1923 Tintown Camp. (Kilmainham Gaol Museum).

As mentioned, a different form of publication which had existed and been in circulation in most of the prisons since 1916 was the prison autograph book and many prisoners used these books as a form of journal as they were passed around, gathering comments, news, poetry and messages of hope for better times. One such autograph book, one of hundreds which survive to the present time, belonged to Mícheál Ua Dúnabháin, Mogeely, County Cork. His book opens with a poem recording the transfer of the prisoners from Cork Female Prison to No. 2 Camp, Tintown: 'We marched that day all stepping proudly/our guard being men who let us down'. The date was recorded as 21 February 1923. Another entry gives an account of conditions:

Prison Life in Tintown
The so-called huts we live in are stables. Each stable is about 56 yards long and eight feet high with an iron roof. The iron partition does not go within a foot of the roof, hence (exposed to) some breezes, rain or whatever is going. In each hut the beds are packed closely together and that makes one's sleep anything but comfortable. Our camp consists of eighteen such huts, two of which are used as dining huts and cookhouses and one for a chapel. You can imagine 1,500 men trying to attend mass there. Occasionally the priest doesn't consider it worth coming. That's his lookout, not ours. The grub, I won't worry you with. Meat? We've another name for it but I won't mention it, one potato each and such a one, black and wet, such is our dinner every day. Shortly after arriving here there were some escapes. The Staters came in force to our camp fully armed and firing, and endeavoured to get the names by roll-call, but there was nothing doing. Our officer issued orders to us not to stand at our beds for inspection and ignore them. In answer to this we were driven out into the open compound at the point of bayonets and kept there all day and to the dark of night without any food or coats …

Other articles are in keeping with the sombre times. There are letters from men on hunger strike. Many contributers added the final messages of comrades who were executed, or remembered the final moments of comrades who had fallen in the fight. Included too, is a copy of a message sent from Seán O'Lehane, OC of Mountjoy, to the mother of Jimmy Mooney after his sudden death:

'He was in perfect health this day week, we thought, when he was suddenly taken ill and we got him to hospital. It was so sudden, the poor fellow was the life of the wing and very well liked by everybody'.

Jimmy Mooney was acting as orderly to the badly-injured Ernie O'Malley and he also took the sudden death of his young friend very badly.

The book records many deaths, reports of meetings, biographies of various republicans, all in different hands and interspersed with these serious articles, poems and a fair smattering of doggerel such as:

> May the Lord above, send down a dove
> with wings as sharp as razors
> to cut the throats of those who vote
> for the damned Free Staters.

How the prisoners viewed Tintown Camp in 1923. Courtesy Caoimhín Caulfield

THE ARGENTA

If the Free State was ruthless in its treatment of prisoners, neither did the Northern state waste any time after partition in seeking to teach republicans and the nationalist community what the future under unionism held in store, and who was going to be in charge. Even before the Civil War, the unionists were preparing for mass imprisonment, and indeed, some prisoners had not even been released from jail at the end of the Tan War when, on 23 May 1922, internment was reintroduced. This came one day after the assassination of the Unionist MP William Twaddell, amid anti-catholic pogroms. Twaddell was founder of the Ulster Imperial Guards, a paramilitary loyalist group claiming 21,000 members.

Early morning swoops in Belfast saw the arrest of thirty-nine men who were brought to Chichester Street Barracks and the following day to Crumlin Road Prison. The unionist regime had declared 24 May 1922 as 'Empire Day'. They were celebrating it as the prisoners were transported across the city, and the prisoners suffered abuse and injury from the mobs as they were trapped in cages on the open-backed tenders.[129] Liam Ó Muireadhaigh, a Belfast Volunteer, was one of those arrested.

> 'That night was spent in B Wing, and next morning in C Wing exercise yard the prison officers attempted to make us walk in single file, like convict prisoners. We refused and so an argument developed. Most of us prisoners stood around debating whether to go back to our cells. While this dispute was proceeding ... the little C Wing gate opened and to our great astonishment in troops about 300 country men from all over the six counties'.[130]

---

129 Ó Muireadhaigh, Liam P. (1946) *Some Reminiscences of Tough Times* Belfast: unpublished manuscript (P.25).

130 Ó Muireadhaigh, Liam P. (1946) *Some Reminiscences of Tough Times* Belfast: unpublished manuscript (P.26).

The earlier attempt at restrictions and imposing penal conditions disappeared and the men began organising, with sport, ranganna Gaeilge, games, concerts. As the summer of 1922 progressed, the sound of war and reports of pogroms from beyond the prison wall in Belfast's battleground streets was the backdrop to the prisoners' lives.

On 4 June 1922 loyalists and B Specials launched gun attacks on the Mater Hospital (adjacent to the jail), based on the false flag that the IRA were using the hospital as a vantage point to attack the prison. In scenes reminiscent of what was happening in Mountjoy with the Free State Army, B Specials fired repeatedly up at the cell windows, though the prisoners suffered no casualties. On 22 June prisoners were taken from their cells at 10.30 pm and ordered to pack their things. They were assembled in a prison hall and beginning around midnight batches of fifty at a time were taken in Crossley tenders from the Crumlin Road to the prison ship, the *S.S. Argenta*.

'The route was lined with Specials almost from Crumlin Rd Prison to the *Argenta*,' wrote Ó Muireadhaigh. 'The last batch went on board around 4.30 am. After all were locked safely the *Argenta* was towed down Belfast Lough to Carrick Roads where she lay at anchor until late September. That morning before sailing all the Derry internees were put on board also.'[131]

The Derry prisoners arrested in the earlier swoops had been interned until then in Derry Gaol.

The *Argenta* was a three-mast wooden ship, built during the First World War in the USA to carry munitions to France. It was unsuitable for its new life as an internment ship, but the 12-foot-barbed wire fence around the deck, and the eight internee 'cages' built below on the first deck, combined with quarters for prison officers and for the armed A and B Special guard force, were all that the unionist government required to declare it a prison. Conditions were grim for the 375 internees, with primitive sanitation (seawater, bilge water and buckets), poor food, little or no medical services and gross overcrowding. In those congested conditions protests by prisoners occurred frequently, and the penalties for such agitation or breach of the rules was often swift and severe. Lacking a specific 'punishment' area, prisoners were often dispatched to Derry Gaol (or to Larne Workhouse which was considered as an annex of the *Argenta*) to a punishment block for any perceived 'offence'. Infringements ranged from organising the teaching of Irish,

---

131 Ó Muireadhaigh, Liam P. (1946) *Some Reminiscences of Tough Times* Belfast: unpublished manuscript (PP. 28-29).

to writing letters about conditions or for fighting with prisoners deemed to be collaborating with the regime or for 'insolence'.

Setting up structures and internal discipline within a body of men who were not all members of any single organisation (the IRA, for example) was no easy task. In addition, the course of the Civil War being fought in the Twenty-Six Counties eventually led to factional physical fighting between the two sides on board the ship:

> Another fact which tended to complicate life on the boat was that a number of men from Northern Ireland had been down south from the start of the Civil War and had taken part in that conflict on one or the other side and after the cessation of warfare in the South, many of these returned to the North from about April 1923. On their arrival North a number of these men were picked up by the Northern authorities and some were sent on to the *Argenta*. Before those men arrived, the Civil strife in the south had caused many bitter disturbances amongst internees on the *Argenta*. Many of the men had taken sides for or against the Treaty, and differences of opinion and disputes on this question caused bitter arguments. This bitterness was much increased and renewed by the arrival of those Civil War participants from both sides amongst us. These men, immediately on their arrival on the boat, started a bitter vendetta against each other. In fact, getting together on the boat afforded an opportunity for them for continuing their previous Civil War fight. To add fuel to this unfortunate position, these new elements attracted partisans to their different sides and many miniature battles *royal* took place from time to time.[132]

An elected councillor from Fermanagh, Cahir Healy, was guilty, it would appear, of fomenting the tension. When news that the republican Chief of Staff, Liam Lynch, had been assassinated by Free State soldiers in April 1923, trouble broke out on the ship.

> 'Cahir Healy was in Cage S2. When they heard about the killing of Liam Lynch, Cahir Healy, he had the newspapers, he gathered the newspapers and lit a bonfire with glee ... and the cage set

---

132 Shiel, John (1954) https://www.militaryarchives.ie/collections/online-collections/bureau-of-military-history-1913-1921/reels/bmh/BMH.WS0928.pdf (P.25).

fire to them and danced around with glee that Liam Lynch had been shot. They didn't know who the man was. None of them had pity ...'[133]

It was little wonder that fighting broke out on board in the face of such provocation.

The Ship's Bulletin

Some prisoners on board were suspected spies and informers and deep divisions arose when a Commission (nicknamed 'The Chat' by the internees) was established by the unionist government. The Commission allowed prisoners to apply for release, but such paroles were to be conditional on making full confessions of previous activity; pledging not to protest against the state in future; agreeing to reside in certain designated areas; and giving information on the IRA. Eventually, a part of the cages was sectioned off to hold men who had participated in the Commission and were awaiting release.

> 'That these men appeared before their commission, which was boycotted by the general body of the prisoners, produced resentment amongst those of us who had been active in the Republican cause. These feelings of resentment against them caused them to be confined in one cage as a safety precaution.'[134]

Organisation on board the ship was, however, maintained and many prisoners learned Irish, music, history and made handicrafts from whatever they could lay their hands on. Liam Ó Muireadhaigh recalled the ship's newspaper created by the prisoners: 'After a short time on the Argenta Messr Healy and Mayne produced a small paper known as *The Ships Bulletin.*'[135]

The Healy in question was the previously mentioned Councillor Cahir Healy, a founding member of Conradh na Gaeilge and of Sinn Féin. He took the pro-Treaty side in the Civil War, thereby accepting partition and recognising the unionist government yet now, ironically,

133   Kleinrichert, Denise (2002) *Argenta* Dublin: Irish Academic Press (P.159).
134   Shiel, John (1954) https://www.militaryarchives.ie/collections/online-
        collections/bureau-of-military-history-1913-1921/reels/bmh/BMH.WS0928.pdf
        (P.24).
135   Ó Muireadhaigh, Liam P. (1946) *Some Reminiscences of Tough Times* Belfast:
        unpublished manuscript (P.38).

found himself interned by that government in the north. He was elected twice as MP for Fermanagh South Tyrone in November 1922 and again in 1923 while still a prisoner on the *Argenta*. His period of internment lasted from May 1922 until February 1924.[136]

James Mayne was an urban councillor, arrested in the first round-up and interned until 1924. He was, for a while, OC of 'neutral' prisoners on the ship and would be accused of helping to break a hunger strike by assisting in preparation of meals in October 1923, earning extra privileges for himself in the process. All that, of course, was in the future and at the time the ship's paper was in existence the troubles of the Civil War had yet to surface on board.

The Ship's Bulletin or *The Bulletin* 'was read out every Monday at 12 o'clock on the deck. The Governor (Drysdale) and Chief and other officials used to come down along the outside of the wire and listen to the week's news. This bulletin was very humorous and slagged everyone including officials. It was gathered from conversations overheard from lads talking during their sleep, from unfavourable love letters, etc and Terry Mackin's dream.'[137]

Terry Mackin was an older prisoner, almost sixty-years-of-age, and owing to bronchial trouble was confined to bed for days and sometimes weeks at a stretch. Terry was said to have had a dream almost every week about men being released: 'He always dreamed that everybody would be released next Monday morning, but his dream never came true.'[138]

Another story in the paper concerned an incident when 'old Harry Dobbin' and a few friends were caught trying to make poitín in the cookhouse. Liam Ó Muireadhaigh wrote that some time after this cookhouse incident 'a number of warders were caught trafficking in whiskey, smuggling alcohol in to the Internees. It was said that seven were discharged.'

Apart from Healy and Mayne other contributors to the *Ship's Bulletin* included Dr Thomas Laverty and Frank Gallagher.[139] Denise Kleinrichert says Gallagher, who became the primary editor of the paper, was accused by the prison authorities of signing a smuggled letter

136   *Dictionary of Irish Biography*: https://www.dib.ie/biography/healy-cahir-a3890.
137   Ó Muireadhaigh, Liam P. (1946) *Some Reminiscences of Tough Times* Belfast: unpublished manuscript (P.38).
138   Ó Muireadhaigh, Liam P. (1946) *Some Reminiscences of Tough Times* Belfast: unpublished manuscript (P.38).
139   Kleinrichert, Denise (2002) *Argenta* Dublin: Irish Academic Press (P.157).

to a public body in the north which had been published in the press. The ship's paper ceased production when he was 'gaoled' for the offence (possibly by transfer to the punishment cells in Derry Gaol).

The last of the internees in the north, post-partition, were released in 1925, but it would be two more years before the last of the sentenced prisoners were freed. These included three men known as 'the Derry Prisoners', jailed for their part in the death of two prison guards in Derry Gaol who had died from an accidentally high dose of chloroform used to knock them out during an abortive escape from the jail the night before the Treaty was signed in 1921. The men had been sentenced to death despite the signing of the Treaty and after a last-minute reprieve had been moved to prison in Scotland and eventually back to Crumlin Road in Belfast in 1926 and freed the following year.

As a footnote to the twenties, the first official prison newspaper in the history of Britain's prison system made its debut when *The Weekly New-sheet* appeared for the first time on 16 December 1929. The paper, produced in the print-shop in Maidstone Prison, was circulated to many other prisons and published every Tuesday. It carried, 'the main items of national and international news and, of course, the football results and league tables which some prisoners considered to be the most important.'[140]

Tom Clarke had, of course, stolen the march on them by almost fifty years.

140   Grew, BD (Major) (1958) *Prison Governor*. London: Herbert Jenkins (P. 86).

Died on Hunge

LEGION OF THE REARGUARD 1924–1970

Tony D'Arcy died on hunger strike on the 16 April 1940

BELFAST AND DERRY JAILS

The thirties in Ireland were, as in much of Europe, merely a lull between wars. Internment of republican prisoners began a few days before Christmas 1938 with the arrest of a dozen or so men in Belfast. Those arrested included the *Argenta* diarist Liam Ó Muireadhaigh who by then was no longer a member of the IRA. However, because he had been observed collecting money to aid prisoners' families that was sufficient pretext to have him arrested in the first swoop and interned without trial for the next seven years.

Just eleven years after the release of the last of the 1920s prisoners, some of those freed then were now hounded and rounded up once again and placed back in D Wing, Crumlin Road. Hundreds more would join Ó Muireadhaigh, with prisoners being held at various stages in prisons in Belfast, Derry, and Armagh and on yet another prison hulk, this one named the *Al Rawdah*. Between 1939 and 1945 a total of 827 men and at least 19 women were interned at different periods in the north.

The internees immediately began securing a set of rights and living conditions distinct from the normal prison regime, and once again began organising their own day-to-day lives. Officially, internees were to be treated in a fashion akin to remand prisoners but in practice they had a much more relaxed regime. Organisation began around the familiar themes of education, Irish classes, planning escapes, handicrafts and inevitably, a prison newspaper.

Faoi Ghlas

Writing in his prison memoir Tarlach Ó hUid recalled that among several publications a newspaper of the name *Faoi Ghlas* had been in circulation in Belfast Prison in the 1920s. The title was now revived and adopted as the primary newspaper among prisoners arrested and interned from 1938–1945 in Crumlin Road Jail and in Derry Jail.

Faoi Ghlas went through different iterations during those years. The paper was started in 1939 as an English language newssheet by Belfast prisoner Peadar Ó Broin. He had the experience before his internment of printing what Ó hUid called a 'sleg sheet', a small local bulletin with local stories and humour and *scéal* in the Lower Falls. When finding himself interned in D Wing, in 'The Crum', Ó Broin decided to re-establish the old title from the twenties and managed to obtain a typewriter on which the wing paper was typed, using carbon paper. This allowed several copies to be circulated. By early 1940 Ó Broin had tired of the effort and offered the paper to Tarlach Billí, the name by which Ó hUid was universally known in prison (aside from the prison authorities who had him in custody under the alias of 'Terence White').

Ó hUid had some experience in newssheets having previously been Director of Publicity for the IRA, editing their paper *War News* and running a pirate Irish republican radio station. By this stage in his life Ó hUid was one of the foremost language activists in the northern IRA. He agreed to take over the prison paper but decided to publish it 'as Gaeilge'. Ó Broin gave Ó hUid the typewriter and carbon paper, and with the help of the artistic Seán de Blanc, a lino-cut masthead for the paper was created, assuring uniformity from edition to edition. A dozen copies of each edition were sold and distributed on the wing, and although *an cló Gaelach* (Gaelic font) was still in use, *Faoi Ghlas* was printed using the typewriter's Roman typeface.

Little did the tunnellers of 1942 going below ground into a disused shaft under D Wing Crumlin Road, suspect that their tunnel would be 'discovered' eighty years later, long after the Crum ceased to be a prison, when renovations were taking place to use the wing as part of a visitor centre.

Ó hUid, throughout this time was Rúnaí and organiser of An Cumann Gaelach, the most active of a plethora of clubs and groups the prisoners had established to cater for various interests in the wing, all of them drawing from the same pool of prisoners and many of them having identical and overlapping membership lists.

Prison life, however, does not exist in a vacuum and soon—because of some non-related tension between prisoners and prison staff—the prison governor, Lance Thompson, ordered the confiscation of the typewriter in what the prisoners viewed as a petty act of punishment.

Some of the prisoners who were interned in Crumlin Road in the 1940s signing the ubiquitous 'autograph book' including Tarlach Billí (editor of *Faoi Ghlas*) and Seán Mac Adaimh (uncle of Gerry Adams) who escaped from Derry Jail. Courtesy of Seán Ó Brolcháin.

The paper continued as a handwritten and hand-copied manuscript until a dispute arose about some of the articles which were critical, or derogatory, towards an Irish dancing class and its teacher. The *múinteoir* took offence and the paper ceased publication when no apologies were forthcoming.

In February 1942, around 200 prisoners—including some who had been moved from Crumlin Road to Derry Jail or to the prison ship *Al Rawdah*—were transferred back to Crumlin Road Prison. The ship had been a grim experience. Around 170 prisoners had been bussed from Derry Jail in September 1941 to the boat, moored off Killyleagh, where they were joined by thirty or forty more from Crumlin Road. Living conditions, food and medical care were all grim and one prisoner, Jack Gaffney (who had been OC in Derry Jail before the move) died of medical neglect when he fell from a bunk. Another ten prisoners would die in the months and years after. Seán Dolan, from Derry, died in October 1942, just eight months after his spell on the Al Rawdah.

When the prison ship was closed, an AGM of the Cumann Gaelach was called for the benefit of all the re-united groups of prisoners. A proposal to resume producing *Faoi Ghlas* found no one willing, as feelings were still raw over the failure to resolve the insult to the dancing teacher.

In the wake of an almost completed tunnel being discovered under D Wing in October 1942, around 200 prisoners were moved, over a space of three weeks, from Belfast to Derry Jail. There, the Cumann Gaelach quickly re-established itself. The dispute over the insult to the dance teacher had still to be settled as the dance teacher initially refused to resume classes in the new prison because of what had been written in *Faoi Ghlas* the previous year. Ironically, the same protagonists in the dispute were all working amicably, or at least without antagonism, on other projects in the wing including ranganna Gaeilge, ranganna ceoil, and planning an escape from the jail.

An Drithleog

Tensions would soon surface again, however, and before long the Cumann Gaelach in Derry Jail agreed to recognise a new sub-committee which styled itself 'An Drithleog' (The Spark). It had begun producing a news sheet of the same name, *An Drithleog,* which was edited by Breandán Ó Baoighill. *An Drithleog* had a rocky beginning, with complaints from the chair of the Cumann Gaelach from the first issue regarding content which attacked the commitment of *Fáinneoirí* (Irish speakers on the wing who had obtained the Fáinne and were therefore obliged to speak Irish on all occasions).

An Drithleog reported that some of them had been overheard speaking in English and were not showing a good example to learners. Another article in the paper launched a sideswipe at the Cumann Gaelach by saying that the new sub-committee and paper would give people a chance to use Irish now, a chance that the Cumann Gaelach hadn't been providing until then. The Cumann Gaelach, of course, refuted this and the editor was called in to a Cumann Gaelach committee meeting on 14 March to explain the articles. He stood over his allegation regarding *Fáinneoirí* not showing example but withdrew his criticism of the Cumann Gaelach and said that it was the previous Cumann (in Belfast) that he had in mind when he wrote the article. A week later on 20 March 1943, the editor, Breandán Ó Baoighill, was one of twenty-one prisoners who dramatically escaped from Derry Jail. The prisoners had tunnelled from a ground floor cell, going down eighteen feet below the eighteenth-century jail walls, digging through an old graveyard and passing under a coffin to emerge in a coal shed in Harding Street.[141]

The amazed Logue family had their breakfast interrupted as one after another of the escapees ran through their kitchen to a waiting lorry which took most of them across the border to Donegal where to their dismay, they were all re-arrested by the Free State Army and interned in the Curragh.

The tunnel had been months in the planning and when the escape was over and the tunnel was being investigated by the RUC, a second tunnel—probably dating from when prisoners had been held there in 1939 and 1940—was found. That tunnel had been abandoned twelve feet below ground when it met the deep foundations of the prison wall; or perhaps the work had been interrupted when the prisoners had been moved with little warning in September 1940 to the Al Rawdah.

After the escape, Pádraig Ó Gallchobhair agreed to take over as editor of *An Drithleog* but over the following months the configurations of the Cumann, and its various sub-committees changed with a new chairperson and completely new committee installed at the AGM.

---

141 Breandán Ó Baoighill died on 25 July 1955 when a bomb he was preparing exploded prematurely. He had broken from the IRA and set up a small organisation called Laochra Uladh.

An Fréamh (The Root), An Chúis (The Cause)

An Drithleog must have been collateral damage during these personel changes because by January 1944 a committee meeting heard that the editor of the prison paper—now called *An Fréamh* (*The Root*)—was resigning as he could not continue without further help from the wing. He asked the committee of Cumann Gaelach to take on the responsibility for the paper. The committee agreed, but changed the name of the paper yet again, to *An Chúis* (*The Cause*). To attract articles a writing competition was announced with a prize of twenty cigarettes. The decision to rename the paper caused some dispute when the full Cumann meeting took place a week later with members arguing that the committee should not have changed the name. However, the chairperson said that the name change was needed to give the paper a fresh start. In an effort to prevent old tensions reviving, or to avoid further insults appearing in its pages, Tarlach Billí was appointed adjudicator as to the future contents in the paper.

The paper was struggling. Two months passed without the proposed new paper appearing and when it finally arrived in March it was decided to give the paper out for free since people had been waiting so long for it. (Ó hUid was later to write that the prison papers the men produced were usually 'sold' for a cigarette in the tobacco currency of life *faoi ghlas*[142].) The editor put the delay down to a lack of assistance and contributions, and names were collected at the committee meeting of the Cumann of prisoners willing to write for the paper. April 1944 saw further difficulties when the editor explained that he could not write fast enough to make all the required copies and that they were trying to see if a 'writing machine' could be found outside the prison. It was wartime, with all the rationing of equipment, paper and other goods and the committee was not in a position to help. At the same meeting he reported, for example, that they had no chalk for the teachers, and no money to buy chalk. Letters were dispatched to Conradh na Gaeilge seeking help.

In August 1944, however, the Derry prison paper would come to an abrupt end as the internees were once more manacled together and driven in buses back to Belfast, guarded by greater numbers of B Specials than there were of prisoners on each bus. The two branches of the Cumann Gaelach from Belfast and Derry met as a re-united Cumann

142   *Inniu* (1975) Samhain 1975 Dublin.

and at their first meeting agreed, among other matters, to re-establish the Belfast prison paper, *Faoi Ghlas*. Tarlach Billí was appointed editor but the paper's days were numbered. World War II was coming to an end and the unionist government had no further pretext for the internment of republicans. The IRA, both inside and outside the prisons, was, in any case, in no real position to wage war.

At a Cumann Gaelach committee meeting in April 1945 *Faoi Ghlas* was mentioned in reference to an article on lists of books in the wing. Ó hUid himself felt that the standard of Irish in the paper had improved: 'Míle b'fhearr a bhí an Ghaeilge a bhí in uimhreacha 1944-45. Lena chois sin bhíodh pictiúirí agam, ghearrainn léaráidí foirsteanacha as seanirisí a bhailínn ó mo chombhraighdeanaigh'.[143] ('The Irish in the paper was a thousand times better in the 1944-45 editions. As well as that, I had pictures now, as I used to cut out suitable illustrations from old magazines that I would collect from my fellow internees.')

An Coimhéadóir (The Screw)

The paper was handwritten, four sheets of card-paper written on one side with two colums of text in pencil and indian ink. Pictures were stuck to the card with prison porridge—far better than any glue, in Ó hUid's opinion. He had by now reverted to the Cló Gaelach once more and copies were posted on the notice board of the wing for everyone to read. Ó hUid recognised that the standard of Irish in his paper was beyond some of his comrades but that gap in proficiency would, in turn, inspire the creation of yet another prison paper, *An Coimhéadóir* (*The Screw*):[144]

'Ní miste a lua go ndearna Liam Mac Conmara aithris orm agus thosaigh ar iris bhalla dá chuid féin a scríobh, *An Coimhéadóir*, do dhaoine nach raibh eolas go leor acu ar an Ghaeilge le m'iarrachtsa a léamh'.[145] ('It's worth mentioning that Liam Mac Conmara followed my example and began writing his own 'wall journal', *An Coimhéadóir*, for those who hadn't enough Irish to read my efforts.')

143   Ó hUid, Tarlach (1985) *Faoi Ghlas* Dublin: FNT (P.226).
144   Coimheadóir does not appear in any of the major Irish dictionaries but it was a word widely used among republican prisoners for prison warders, or screws.
145   Ó hUid, Tarlach (1985) *Faoi Ghlas* Dublin: FNT (P.227).

Tarlach Ó hUid was one of the last of the forties' internees to be released in the North, in December 1945. It goes without saying that he spent the remainder of his days working in the Irish language newspaper industry.

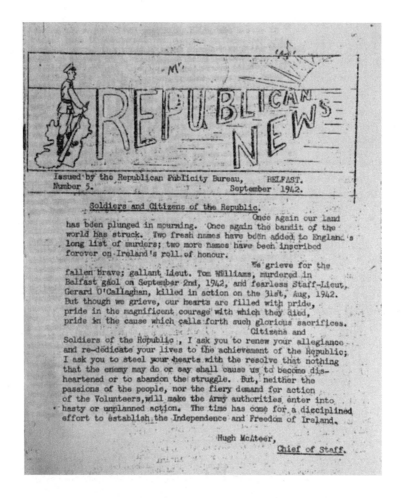

The tradition of the mosquito press continued long after the 1920s. This September 1942 *Republican News*, banned under the Special Powers Act, carried a tribute to IRA Volunteers Tom Williams and Gerard O'Callaghan. Courtesy of Sinn Féin.

TINTOWN, TAKE TWO

Internees and sentenced prisoners were also held during the years of what, in the Twenty-Six Counties, was called The Emergency. They were interned mainly in the Curragh, but sentenced prisoners were also held in Arbour Hill, Mountjoy and in Portlaoise (Maryborough) prisons. In April 1940 Jack McNeela and Tony D'Arcy died (in St Bricin's Military Hospital) on a hunger strike they had begun in March to secure political treatment for two comrades being held in Mountjoy without political recognition. In May of 1946, Seán McCaughey also made the supreme sacrifice when he died after twenty-two days on hunger and thirst strike in Portlaoise Prison. The conditions the prisoners were held under in Portlaoise were inhumane, in Arbour Hill and Mountjoy oppressive and in the Curragh depressing. The Curragh was riven with splits among the prisoners during the 1940s, with three distinct groups at one point among the internees some of whom ostracised members of the other two groups.

The splits were possibly festering below the surface for some time and arose from a change of leadership in the Army Council outside the prison which some saw as an overthrow of the previous leadership. De Valera's government, a body of men and women once hunted into the hills by the Free State government, now ruthlessly hunted down their former republican comrades who still refused to accept the Free State as a republican solution. The IRA, North and South, was in disarray. While members of the 'new' leadership were arrested and sent to Arbour Hill on IRA membership charges, conditions down in the Curragh deteriorated: complaints about inedible food, and cold, leaking huts and living accommodation went unanswered. Máirtín Ó Cadhain described it as Ireland's Siberia. His Arbour Hill comrades described their cells as the coldest place in Ireland. The Army Council had almost to a man been arrested in a swoop in 1939 and sentenced to terms in Arbour Hill. On completion of their sentences they were interned in the Curragh.

One short-lived newspaper was produced during the last few months of 1940 in Arbour Hill by Séamus Ó Goilidhe. In an interview with Uinseann MacEoin, Séamus recalled learning Irish and German in

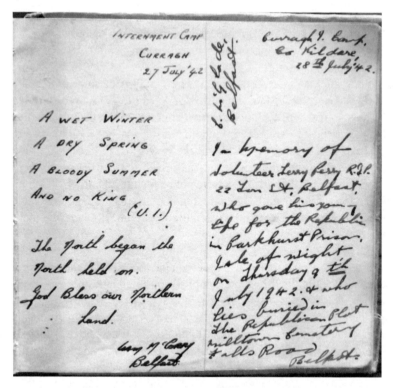

In another Curragh autograph book, some prisoners from Belfast left their mark. Charlie McGlade references the death of Terry Perry, who died of medical neglect in Parkhurst Prison, 1942

Arbour Hill with Pádraig Mac Caomhánach. The regime was strict and the men were cut off from news from the outside world. He said: 'There were no newspapers or radio in the jail, current events being cut from letters. So I started a small journal composed from snippets, from rumour and from my imagination, and bolstered it with hand-drawn maps. It ran for a while until December when we were due for 'release', meaning automatic internment, being then transferred by covered lorry to the Curragh.'[146]

Shortly after their arrival, they deposed the Camp OC who they believed had allowed a regime to exist where the prisoners were treated as less than POWs. Their decision and the authority to depose the OC was in some way based on the 'rank' held by the Chief of Staff before

146   Ó Goilidhe, Séamus, in MacEoin, Uinseann (1997) *The IRA in the Twilight Years 1923-1948*. Dublin: Argenta Publications (P.710).

his arrest but a large group of prisoners felt that the new OC and his Adjutant had no right to assume leadership based on their outside rank since IRA volunteers customarily lost their rank on arrival in prison. Dissension took root.

Soon after taking over control, the new staff made some immediate changes. Gearóid Ó Maoilmhichíl, writing in the 1970s, recalled that the new staff stopped some education courses, on the bizarre grounds that the prisoners were becoming both too socialist and too involved in the Irish language.[147] To be fair to the new staff, in later years they would explain that they believed that conditions in the camp were deteriorating and that prisoners were not being treated fairly by the Free Staters nor were the authorities treating the men as political prisoners, but as criminals.[148] Their upheaval of the status quo was therefore more of a duty than a choice.

Their next decision, however, had longer term consequences: they ordered prisoners to set fire to a specified hut as a protest against further reductions which had just been applied to the already meagre butter rations. This order was given against the appeals of prisoners who had spent much longer in the camp and who had created a system of tunnels connecting the huts in preparation for an escape. When the first hut was set ablaze the fire accidently spread to other huts, burning them to the ground and the scorched earth revealed the elaborate tunnel network to the Free State guards, who were as inflamed at this discovery as they had been at the burning of the huts earlier. Two days of brutality followed. Prisoners were crowded into the remaining, unburnt huts which had neither bedding or heating and were kept locked there without food or water for almost three days. On the first day out of the huts after this lock-up, 16 December 1940, prisoners queued for breakfast and as they approached the canteen hut a Póilín Airm (Military Policeman) opened fire, killing Barney Casey, a prisoner from Longford. He was shot in the back. Four other prisoners were wounded: Máirtín Standún (who was shot in the face), Walter Mitchell, Bob Flanagan, and Art Moynihan. The prisoners' leaders were forced to run the gauntlet of baton-wielding Military Police from the cage to the punishment block known as 'The Glasshouse', being ferociously assaulted all along the way. Little wonder the prisoners euphemistically called this journey 'the mahogany road'. There, they were charged with

---

147   Ó Maoilmhichíl, Gearóid (1975): *Cuimhní Géibhinn (1940-1943). Dublin:* Leas, Earrach 1975.

148   Quearney, Christy in MacEoin, Uinseann (1997) *The IRA in the Twilight Years 1923-1948.* Dublin: Argenta Publications (P.782).

destroying the prison huts and faced trial before the Military Courts. They were found guilty and sentenced to various terms of up to ten years in prison.

Back in the main camp, prisoners tried to fend for themselves and forage fuel for the stoves in the remaining huts. A dispute arose between groups of prisoners when Tadhg Lynch, the OC of what was known as 'the Cork hut', accepted coal from the Free State guards. Other prisoners believed that this action was a breach of orders. The dispute escalated into a split with one side refusing to speak to the other, a situation which continued for years, and which eventually led to the further splitting of prisoners who agreed with neither side.

Splanc

Somewhere among all this tension small newspapers appeared. 'The Connolly Group' in the prison camp, produced a journal called *Splanc*. Michael O'Riordan, from the West Cork Gaeltacht, grew up in Cork City where he joined the Fianna and the IRA. He joined the Communist Party of Ireland in 1935 while still in the IRA and in 1936 was part of the Connolly Column which went to fight fascism in Spain, fighting on all fronts and being wounded at Ebro. Ó Riordán was for a time OC of the hut populated by Cork prisoners, and was centrally involved in education, both his own and others. He learned Russian and Irish in the camp, later saying that he had learned the two most important languages on earth. With the group he had affiliated to, the Connolly group, founded by the Communist internee Neil Gould, he published a paper named *Splanc*.

Seamus Ronayne recalled: 'The Connolly Group issued a magazine for a short while in the Camp, the name *Splanc* or *Spark* was derived of course from Lenin's little paper *Iskra,*[149] published in Munich in 1900. I wrote one article for *Splanc* about the influence of Marxism on the Modern world.'[150] Another Irish word for spark is *Drithleog*, which was—as mentioned earlier—the name of a prison paper in Derry in 1944, although that prison paper had no left-wing connections.

Gould was suspected of arguing the communist cause in the prison and in this he was gaining support. There was growing disillusionment with organised religion as the prisoners identified the chaplain with their

149   *Iskra* – Spark.
150   Ronayne, Seamus in MacEoin, Uinseann (1997) *The IRA in the Twilight Years 1923-1948*. Dublin: Argenta Publications (P.805).

jailers (as indeed the chaplain himself did) and prisoners in the Curragh were excommunicated until they renounced the IRA. Gould held a lively and well-attended Russian class in the camp which only ended when he was accused by Ó Cadhain and others of teaching Soviet propaganda as part of the weekly lessons. Soviet Russia supported the Allies against the Axis and some republicans found it unpalatable that they were being asked to support Britain via this back door.

Another newly-arrived prisoner, Belfast's Harry White, was asked by Liam Leddy, the OC of the main IRA group which he joined to keep an eye on Gould and the Connolly Group and report back on anything they were writing. He refused. He also said: 'I did not agree with certain communists in there who, when Russia was dragged into the war, said it was our duty to go and join the British Army. Those who were loudest with that sort of talk made sure themselves not to join ...'[151] Harry eventually moved out from that group to a non-aligned group of prisoners.

In 1942 Neil Gould was released from internment after an unprecedented appeal from Pearse Kelly, the OC of one of the IRA factions, to Catholic Primate, Cardinal MacRory to secure Gould's freedom to save the souls of the (Catholic) prisoners who were coming under Gould's communist influences.

Barbed Wire

The other paper circulating in Tintown was *Barbed Wire*. Once again, an older prison journal name was revived as *Barbed Wire* which had previously been used for the prison paper in the internment camp of Ballykinlar. Derry Kelleher remembered in an interview with Uinseann Mac Eoin that, 'Michael Kelly (who with Máirtín Ó Cadhain had been providing lectures to the prisoners) induced in me also a flair for writing, encouraging me to produce my first article dealing with science and socialism and published in our replicated *Barbed Wire*.'[152] According to Cathal Ó hÁinle, 'Ó Cadhain also edited the prison journal, *Barbed Wire,* and contributed material in Irish and English to it, including songs which he had translated into Irish, such as "The Red Flag" and "The Internationale" and more homely Irish ballads.'[153]

151   White, Harry & MacEoin, Uinseann (1985) *Harry.* Dublin: Argenta (P.93).
152   Kelleher, Derry in MacEoin, Uinseann (1997) *The IRA in the Twilight Years 1923-1948.* Dublin: Argenta Publications (P. 647).
153   Ó hÁinle, Cathal (2002) *Máirtín Ó Cadhain, Aitheasc Luan na Trionóide* Dublin.

Christy Quearney mentioned in his later interviews a similar small magazine in Mountjoy during those years: 'Seamus Murphy was writing for *The Bell,* and I was doing a bit of scribbling myself with Seamus as my editor. In 1941 Seamus asked me to do an article for the Mountjoy paper. My piece was on republicanism, but I was later to see in the paper that he claimed it as "the best article we have had from any source, and we hope to see a lot more from this contributor". I did not wish, however, to be tied down writing articles for the jail news sheet.'[154]

The 1940s were, of course, the heyday of Seán Ó Faoláin and Peadar O'Donnell's literary magazine, *The Bell.* But in correspondence published in *Brendan Behan: A Life* by Michael O'Sullivan (1999) it is clear that the Prisons' Section in the Department of Justice had ordered the Prison Governor, Seán Kavanagh, to allow material from Behan to be permitted out strictly *for criticism only,* and even then after internal prison censorship and reference-up to the prisons' department. No material by prisoners was to be published. The question arises, therefore, of what paper Seamus Murphy was editing. Since no material from prisoners was permitted for publication outside the prison, Christy Queaney and Seamus Murphy's paper, in Mountjoy, may also have adopted the name *The Bell.* Nothing remains of these papers now, sadly, sometimes not even a name.

Máirtín Ó Cadhain eventually removed himself from the IRA command structure after several years of disagreements over minor matters, policy matters and personal matters. Ó Cadhain—or as the military authorities had it, Internee Coyne—had been interned for a few months in 1939 and released with others when the internment orders were found to be invalid. His friend, fellow countyman and comrade, Tony D'Arcy died on hunger strike, as has been mentioned, in April 1940, and Ó Cadhain had the honour of giving the oration at the funeral in Donaghpatrick cemetery. The ceremony was attacked by the Special Branch with unprecedented violence and many were injured. Ó Cadhain was arrested shortly afterwards in Headford and once again interned. He was named as a suspect in the December 1939 raid on the Armoury in Phoenix Park which netted over a million rounds of ammunition for the IRA, as no less than thirteen lorry-loads of armaments were removed from the building over the space of an hour. Most of the weaponry and bullets were recovered by Gardaí as the IRA struggled to find dumps large enough to accommodate the huge haul of munitions.

154 Quearney, Christy in MacEoin, Uinseann (1997) *The IRA in the Twilight Years 1923-1948.* Dublin: Argenta Publications (P.783).

Ó Cadhain stayed with the main IRA group through the initial splits and as some reconciliation developed in 1943 (during a hunger strike being led by members of an opposing group) he eventually began giving political/economic lectures. His political stance—which advocated a form of Christian or moral distribution of wealth did not appeal to the left-wing prisoners, while his view that armed struggle was achieving nothing enraged the traditional and militaristic prisoners who accused him of turning against the IRA. His teaching of politics ended with threats of an IRA Court of Inquiry and he was suspended, eventually. In time, he sought permission from the prison authorities to set up another non-aligned hut of around thirty men, and further alienated his old comrades by asking for a writing desk and chair, with paper and pens to continue his writing career. This new configuration of prisoners included a re-formed Irish language hut, with prisoners drawn from the existing Irish-speaking huts established as far back as 1941. Already a published author prior to his imprisonment, Ó Cadhain produced more stories during his final years in Tintown some of which were approved for publication by the Special Branch but refused publication by the Military authorities who feared a precedent was being set. This was, ironically, at a time when Ó Cadhain's pre-prison work was being re-printed, at state expense.

In harsh conditions, with repeated searches, regular disturbances, and years of internment without visits, it is little wonder that the prison papers composed in Tintown have vanished without trace. But even in these old prison recollections it is clear that the content of the papers in the 1940s was more than light-hearted banter and satirising of fellow prisoners. Articles on Marxism, science, socialism and republicanism reflected a body of prisoners developing ideology and educating themselves, with some of them returning to the struggle after their release.

It was also a time of cultural struggle. In 1942 a prisoner, Seán Óg Ó Tuama, had been elected President of Conradh na Gaeilge. Ó Tuama's father had been OC of the same prison during the Civil War. His sister Máire was in Mountjoy serving a five-year sentence for her republican activities. Apart from Ó Tuama, other Irish teachers included Peadar McAndrews and Gearóid Ó Maoilmhichíl, considered to be great teachers and very approachable,[155] and of course Máirtín Ó Cadhain. Ó Cadhain could be less patient than the other teachers, some of who were described by him, years later, as: 'Daoine nárbh í an mhúinteoireacht a

155 Dolan, Joe in MacEoin, Uinseann (1997) *The IRA in the Twilight Years 1923-1948.* Dublin: Argenta Publications (P.487).

ngairm ach a mheas gur seirbhís d'Éirinn é an Ghaeilge a mhúine, go díreach mar a dhéanfaidís saighdiúreacht neamhcheirdiúil le seanghunnaí d'Éirinn.'[156]

Together, these and other múinteoirí Gaeilge in the camp helped to produce a new generation of language activists from within the prison population. Some of these gaeilgeoirí would in time be active in the language movements and organisations, men such as Eamonn Ó Cianáin from Belfast who remained a language activist for the next fifty years. Some, however, would find themselves destined to be teaching Irish in prisons again, in the 1950s, 1960s and 1970s.

The Crum

The epicentre of northern imprisonment in the 1950s was Crumlin Road Jail once again. Republicans were also interned in the Curragh during *Operation Harvest* (the 'border campaign') but The Crum had hundreds of prisoners, both internees and sentenced prisoners, in A Wing and D Wing from 1954 until the early 1960s. There was also one woman interned in Armagh Jail.

An invaluable source of information for this period are the prison diaries of Eamonn Boyce, one of eight prisoners arrested after an IRA raid for weapons on a British Army barracks in Omagh in October 1954. Boyce was sentenced to twelve years, on charges of Treason Felony. The Treason Felony Act, introduced at the time of the Young Ireland Movement in 1848, was designed to make the conviction of republicans easier. Prior to this, the charge of treason called for the death penalty on conviction, which juries were reluctant to impose. By adding 'felony' and by replacing the penalty of execution with the option of imposing sentences of up to life imprisonment, convictions were easier to secure. It was treason felony to 'compass, imagine, invent, devise, or intend' to deprive 'the Sovereign' of his crown: to levy war against the sovereign, or to 'move or stir' any foreigner to invade the United Kingdom or any other country belonging to 'the Sovereign'.[157]

Being convicted of treason felony (in addition to the primary charge) meant being sentenced to a longer term in prison than would have occurred under that initial charge.

156   Ó Cathasaigh, Aindrias (2002) *Ag Samhlú Troda*. Dublin: Coiscéim 2002 (*Turgna Teagaisc*: a talk given by Ó Cadhain to the Primary Teachers Union in 1968. (P.84)) 'People who weren't teachers by profession but who believed it was a service to Ireland to teach Irish in the same way they would soldier unprofessionally for Ireland with old guns'. (My translation).

157   https://en.wikipedia.org/wiki/Treason_Felony_Act_1848

In December 1956, two years into his twelve-year sentence, Boyce began keeping a secret diary written in Irish in a small annual diary which was printed by Conradh na Gaeilge. Initially beginning as an exercise to practice his Irish writing skills the diary soon became a brief record of life in the wing. He continued these diaries faithfully, keeping his secret journal hidden from constant searches, until September 1962 when he smuggled the set of chronicles out shortly before his release. The pages were not seen again for the next forty-five years until they were published—in an English translation—by Anna Bryson in 2008.[158]

Boyce and his small group of comrades lived an isolated existence in Crumlin Road during their first couple of years in prison, being the only republicans in the jail. The IRA border campaign did not begin until 1956 and his diary then began recording arrest after arrest. Soon, there were numbers enough of republican prisoners in the wing to begin organising, educating, and securing rights. In January 1957 the Stormont government re-introduced internment (with the South following suit in July). Boyce was not directly affected since his term of imprisonment stretched another five or six years before him, but sentenced prisoners in A Wing, on completion of shorter sentences during the years of internment, were routinely re-arrested and shifted to D Wing as internees.

D Wing began to fill up, with many 'old hands' of the forties' campaign—both ex-internees and former sentenced prisoners, like Joe Cahill—now walking the same well-trodden prison yards once again.

Life as an internee was very different to Cahill's previous experience of incarceration, a time when for weeks he had been held in the death cell awaiting execution. Cahill and four others had their sentence to hang commuted just five days before their comrade, Tom Williams, walked to the gallows. Joe Cahill and the others then spent the following seven years in Crumlin Road as sentenced prisoners, denied political recognition: 'Jail is jail and is never pleasant,' recalled Cahill, 'but I have to say life as an internee was much preferable to that of a convicted prisoner. We had the run of D Wing. The cell doors were opened in the morning, and you were left to your own devices all day.'[159]

---

158 Bryson, Anna (2008) *The Insider: The Belfast Prison Diaries of Eamonn Boyce, 1956–1962*. Dublin: Lilliput Press.

159 Anderson, Brendan (2002) *Joe Cahill. A Life in the IRA*. Dublin: The O'Brien Press (P.146).

This free time and a drive for ranganna Gaeilge and other education soon led to the arrival of a prison paper, *An Braighdeán*. In March 1958, Boyce wrote a diary entry expressing delight that he had managed to smuggle a copy across to A Wing from his internee comrades in D Wing: 'I saw the newspaper called *An Braighdeán* that has been put out by D Wing and it is very good. There is not a word of English in it and I think it has made great strides with the Irish.'[160]

However, while some prisoners were busy creating papers or teaching classes, others—in all likelihood the same activist prisoners—were on the alert for weaknesses in the system. Trouble was always simmering below the surface and two days after he wrote that diary entry he was reporting that a tunnel had been found in D Wing. Joe Cahill later recalled that the internees had 'discovered that an air shaft ran behind the wall in Proinsias MacAirt's end cell, from the basement boiler room to the roof-space above the third floor. A hole was knocked in the cell wall and the shaft was used as the basis for an escape tunnel. Work had been going on for some time and was within three weeks of completion.'[161]

In the ensuing search and the attempt to capture the tunnelers many prisoners were injured, and trouble continued for some days while families who were protesting at the gates of the prison were also attacked. Eventually things in the prison settled down again. Boyce was able to continue smuggling Irish books and papers, which the internees were permitted, across to the stricter regime prevailing among the sentenced prisoners in A Wing.

During those years the men in A Wing, too, produced a paper from time to time. In May 1958 Boyce mentioned that: 'A newspaper was started but there was no Irish in the first issue.'[162] Boyce was never reticent about objecting to things he disagreed with and quite possibly the lack of Irish led to a written protest. In February 1959 Boyce wrote, 'Fuarthas cóip de'n *Sinn Féiner* ar maidin, ach is dóigh liom gur chuir Tomás an gearán fé chois.' ('I received a copy of *The Sinn Féiner* this morning but I suppose Tomás [Mitchel, the Wing OC] has suppressed my complaint.'

160   Bryson, Anna (2008) *The Insider: The Belfast Prison Diaries of Eamonn Boyce, 1956–1962*. Dublin: Lilliput Press (P.152).

161   Anderson, Brendan (2002) *Joe Cahill. A Life in the IRA*. Dublin: The O'Brien Press. (P.148).

162   Bryson, Anna (2008) *The Insider: The Belfast Prison Diaries of Eamonn Boyce, 1956–1962*. Dublin: Lilliput Press (P.164).

A few months later he was writing that 'I spent the whole night writing an article for the paper'[163] but it's likely that he was contributing by now to *An Braighdeán* since he says he 'sent the note *over* this evening.' In October he again mentions a short article, in Irish, for the paper and again in November 'I wrote a good deal for the paper tonight.'[164] Éamon Boyce had built up smuggling routes (lines) in the prison which carried comms from A Wing to D Wing, and through out his eight years in prison his diaries make constant coded references to smuggled letters, messages, cameras, radios, batteries and watches.

An Timire, Saoirse

It was in August 1959 that the sentenced prisoners' Cumann Gaelach took the decision to begin an Irish language paper which they named *An Timire,* and Boyce was appointed editor. He felt that it was a sign of the Irish gaining an interest among the younger prisoners. By October 1961 another new paper was being discussed among the prisoners. It would be named *Saoirse* and the editor was Dáithí Ó Conaill, by now a sentenced prisoner in The Crum after escaping four years earlier from The Curragh. Eamonn Boyce wrote a piece for the first edition on the subject of the Brehon Laws and planned to write another article on the GAA. The course of *Saoirse* was not all plain sailing, however. In November an article by Eamonn Timoney titled 'Quo Vadis Hibernia?' was attacked at a staff meeting in the wing by Seán Garland. In the January 1962 issue Dáithí Ó Conaill refused to print an article by the previous OC of the Wing, Tony Meade, in *Saoirse,* 'because it was indecent'. Although Boyce continued to write for the paper, when he received his copy on 11 January, he wrote: 'I read *Saoirse* tonight—full of crap. I wrote a reply to one article in it, but I don't know if my letter will be published as it's very critical of the author of the article.'[165] The following day he noted that, 'my name wasn't allowed on my article for *Saoirse.*'

163 Bryson, Anna (2008) *The Insider: The Belfast Prison Diaries of Eamonn Boyce, 1956–1962.* Dublin: Lilliput Press (P.180).

164 Bryson, Anna (2008) *The Insider: The Belfast Prison Diaries of Eamonn Boyce, 1956–1962.* Dublin: Lilliput Press (P.199).

165 Bryson, Anna (2008) *The Insider: the Belfast Prison Diaries of Eamonn Boyce, 1956–1962.* Dublin: Lilliput Press (P.390).

Tensions were simmering. At the end of January Boyce 'wrote the first article for a series on history and the republic for publication in *Saoirse*.' A few days later he says: 'Dáithí Ó Conaill [who by now Boyce was disparagingly referring to as 'Mise Éire'] doesn't want to talk to me because the article I wrote for *Saoirse* didn't please him. A note from the OC saying that we must all work together.'[166]

Boyce continued to write for *Saoirse* until his release, but his last two articles were in English as he believed 'the crowd in here don't read the Irish articles'. In May, he wrote an article on Eoghan Rua Ó Súilleabháin and in June he wrote his final article for the paper. By the time Boyce was freed a few months later he had completed eight years in prison. The internees were long gone and their little paper, *An Braighdeán*, was only a memory. *Saoirse,* too, would come to an end as the last of the prisoners were freed shortly after Eamon Boyce returned to Dublin. Such freedom as existed for nationalists in the Six Counties was merely a case of the unionists resting on their oars.

Less than seven years would pass before the power of internment would be invoked once more and the prisons would fill again.

Derry's now demolished jail in Bishop Street. Courtesy of Michael Burns

166   Bryson, Anna (2008) *The Insider: the Belfast Prison Diaries of Eamonn Boyce, 1956–1962*. Dublin: Lilliput Press (P.393).

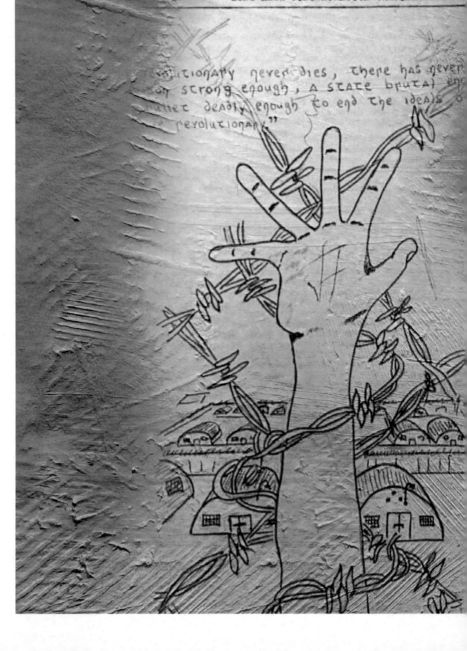

uascailt

JOURNAL OF THE REPUBLICAN P.O.W.'s, C.Coy. (
LONG KESH CONCENTRATION CAMP.

"...tionary never dies, there has never
...on strong enough, a state brutal en...
...llet deadly enough to end the ideals ...
revolutionary."

LAST EDITIONS
1970–2000

Fuascailt, a Long Kesh prison paper

YEARS OF THE LONG WAR

Less than seven years after the last sentenced prisoners were released in 1964, internment was re-introduced in the Six Counties in a series of widespread mass raids and arrests which began around 4 am on 9 August 1971. It was Unionist Groundhog Day. Hundreds of prisoners were brutalised, including a small group (known as the Hooded Men) who were subjected to torture, hooding, sensory deprivation and other brutalities. The initial internees were brought, once more, to Crumlin Road Jail and to a prison ship moored in Belfast Lough, *The Maidstone*. Armagh Jail was also used for a time.

Two former disused RAF airfields—Long Kesh and Magilligan—were also converted into prison camps. Former 'visitors' to Long Kesh when it was a WWII airfield and Air Training Corps centre included the British king and queen and their daughter, the future Queen Elizabeth II; General Eisenhower, and Field Marshal Montgomery. US forces, on the other hand, who were based in the north had their own morale boosting visits with Bob Hope, Tony Romano, Jack Pepper, and Al Jolson. Such are the spoils of war.

However, Long Kesh will go down in history not only because of internment but also because it was the place where British attempts to defeat the republican struggle suffered an irreparable defeat—albeit at great cost—in the 1981 hunger strike, the effects of which reverberate to this very day.

On 19 September 1971 in a series of helicopter lifts from Crumlin Road Jail and the Maidstone, 219 internees were moved to Long Kesh's Nissen huts (arranged on the old runways in barrack-like compounds—which republicans soon referred to as cages). They were used to accommodate the increasing numbers of nationalists and republicans being interned—around 1,600 in total over four years. The huts were named after the designer, Major Peter Nissen, a US-born, British WWI engineer. They were semi-cylindrical in shape and made of corrugated steel and purportedly could be erected by sappers in just four hours. As

132

Early cages in Long Kesh. Cage after cage was rapidly constructed along disused concrete runways on the former RAF base.

a barracks they were extremely draughty and virtually impossible to keep heated.

In 1972 more cages were opened when, after a hunger strike in Crumlin Road (see below), sentenced prisoners successfully secured political status (which the British, trying to salvage something from the republican victory, deftly renamed *special category* status). This was not the only name change. Throughout the world the name Long Kesh was infamously associated with prison cruelty and injustice, and so in late 1972 the British renamed it HMP Maze (or The Maze) in an attempt to escape that opprobrium. However, republicans have always referred to it as Long Kesh, the Kesh, and, later, the H-Blocks of Long Kesh. The H-Blocks, which opened in September 1976, were separated from the cages by a huge wall and were part of a strategy aimed at criminalising the prisoners and the struggle for freedom and independence. Those arrested and convicted after 1 March 1976 were refused political status, were sent to the H-Blocks and were designated as criminals. It was here that the administration stripped prisoners naked, beat them and deprived them of their human rights over many years, all in an attempt to break them.

The brutality failed to break the resolve of the prisoners—the blanket men—and the criminalisation strategy was ultimately defeated, but at a high cost and huge sacrifice. A similar refusal to be criminalised by the republican women in Armagh (where compliance with prison work was required but without the added stigma of wearing a prison uniform) also led to a lengthy protest, solitary confinement and loss of remission.

In the prison hospital in the H-Blocks in 1981 ten prisoners died in a seventh-month long hunger strike which followed an earlier strike. The long prison battle transformed the struggle and led to the electoral rise of Sinn Féin as a major force for change in Irish politics.

Barbed Wire Bulletin

The internees in Long Kesh—including veteran republicans from the 1940s and 1950s with vast prison experience in organising, escaping, and undermining officialdom—soon established traditional command structures. They had their own separate regime to organise their daily lives around recreation, education, political and cultural activities.

In January 1972 internees who were associated with the 'Official' IRA produced the first jail journal from Long Kesh. Internees from both sides of the 1970 republican split were initially held in the same cages. The split had divided the Movement into two groups, which were dubbed 'Provos' and 'Stickies', or more formally, the Provisionals (who became the mainstream Movement) and the Officials. The latter group's political influence and support later completely withered.

While the twelve-page paper was called *Barbed Wire Bulletin* and used an aerial picture of the early Long Kesh cages on its front page, it was not a jail journal in the conventional sense, since it mainly focussed on outside politics, recruitment notices and a copy of a telegram of support for the internees from the Republican Clubs branch in University College, Galway. The content for the paper was smuggled out of the prison and printed and sold outside. Conditions in the prison were covered in an article titled 'Ulster's Shame', which recounted ailments among prisoners, poor food, lack of heating and waterlogged cages. The unionist Prime Minister Brian Faulkner was the *bête noir* of the paper.

In a series of 'letters' written from Long Kesh in the following months, Des O'Hagan (a leading member of the Officials) wrote a weekly column published in the *Irish Times* detailing conditions and life in the internment camp. O'Hagan had been imprisoned previously in A Wing, Crumlin Road, in the 1950s, after being arrested during an attempt to rescue a prisoner undergoing treatment in Belfast's Royal Victoria Hospital. The prisoner had, as it happened, already been released from custody by the time O'Hagan arrived but he and another man were sentenced to four years for possession of a handgun. While imprisoned as a member of what the republican prisoners referred to as the Unit, O'Hagan held the role of Irish teacher for a while in 1957.[167] He began teaching soon after his arrival in June but by October he had left the Unit, apparently after defying a direct order from the Wing OC not to listen to a soccer match on the radio. In January 1958 his troubles continued when he was scalded in a canteen fight.

It was clear to the Stormont government that the border campaign was foundering. It put forward a proposal it knew would be divisive, and in some cases tempting: a process to assess the threat level posed by individual prisoners. The republican prison staff understandably issued an order for the scheme to be boycotted, suspecting that it was designed to offer early release in exchange for cooperation and allow the government to project a conciliatory image. Such schemes existed as far back as the Sankey Commission post-1916, and were resurrected again in 1973 with Long Kesh Commissioners—English judges—brought over to assess whether individual internees should be released (on the basis that they cooperated). Similar inducements were offered to those on the Argenta ship, to those in Crumlin Road and Derry Jails in the 1940s and now once again in the 1950s. The South made similar offers to prisoners to 'sign out'—that is, repudiate the republican struggle.

According to Eamonn Boyce's diaries, Des O'Hagan was one of two prisoners freed several weeks after being interviewed by a notorious RUC Special Branch officer named Fannin. Those in the Crum who engaged with the RUC were treated with suspicion in the wings, whether or not they had compromised themselves.

---

167 Bryson, Anna (2008) *The Insider: The Belfast Prison Diaries of Eamonn Boyce, 1956–1962*. Dublin: Lilliput Press (P.99).

The weekly *Irish Times'* articles O'Hagan penned in 1972 were eventually published in book form forty years after his release as *Letters from Long Kesh.*[168]

An Eochair

In 1973 *An Eochair* (*The Key*) was compiled, for the most part, by sentenced prisoners connected to the Official IRA in the prison, while the *Barbed Wire Bulletin* had been the paper of Official IRA internees. *An Eochair* was published and on sale outside the wire and was described as 'A Bulletin of the Irish Republican Movement, Long Kesh'. The choice of the title *An Eochair* was explained by a caption below the masthead which declared: 'The Key to True Freedom – Socialism'. A publishing blurb inside the paper stated: 'This is a newspaper published by the republican prisoners in Cage 21, Long Kesh. Its contents serve as an insight into Western Europe's only concentration camp while at the same time giving the prisoners' view on the "outside" situation.'

The May 1973 edition of the paper contained some poetry; a couple of cartoons about prison food; details of the harassment of visitors; an article over-optimistically seeing the UDA and William Craig's Vanguard movement as potentially leading 'the Protestant working class' towards socialism; a prisoner list, and an appeal to supporters to purchase handicrafts made in Long Kesh to keep the prison co-op in funds.

For the next four years the paper would be published three or four times yearly and the content remained consistent. There were articles wistfully philosophising about Protestant working-class awakening; features satirising Governor Hilditch (often deliberately misspelt as Hillbitch); articles describing life in the prison, visits, food, education, and expressions of international solidarity. Snippets which historians might find useful included a 1975 price list for handicrafts from the prisoners' co-op: Gents [sic] Wallets were £3.50; a Celtic Cross was £5 and a harp was £6.

In July 1973, fourteen months after the Official IRA had called a ceasefire, just over forty of that organisation's prisoners remained in the Cages of Long Kesh and their numbers—and existence—stagnated. The rhetoric of the paper was far more militant and anti-state than the

168   O'Hagan, Des (2012) *Letters from Long Kesh*. Dublin: Citizen Press.

The prison paper of the sentenced Official IRA prisoners. Some 1970s'
Long Kesh papers were printed and sold outside the camp.

actions of their organisation outside the prison. Conversely—at least in the early years—occasional articles reflecting prison solidarity appeared: for example, when the prison was burnt down in 1974; or in some articles supporting the Price sisters who, with Gerry Kelly and Hugh Feeney, had suffered horrific force-feeding on hunger strike in England.

In the 1975–76 period, bullish declarations were made about fighting to protect political status: 'We Will Not Barter Political Status' declared one headline. Later articles were more antagonistic and dismissive of 'the Provos'. Despite the vow never to 'barter' status, their remaining prisoners would be the first group to abandon the hard-earned political status in the cages, agree to be transferred and to conform to the prison regime in Crumlin Road in exchange for promised release in the mid-1980s. Further afield, a magazine named *Drithleog* was published in the USA by supporters of the 'officials' and contained articles which were mainly written by prisoners although left-wing rhetoric and articles supportive of revolutionary groups in other countries which appeared for Irish consumption in *An Eochair* were discreetly absent from the US periodical.

Long Kesh Hut 60 Bulletin

As the number of internees and cages increased, and with the arrival of sentenced prisoners, cages started to be designated according to which political grouping was the more dominant. Mainstream republicans—Provos, in mediaspeak—tended to make up the majority. The two main loyalist factions (the UVF and the UDA/UFF) also had separate cages.

However, each new cage was almost identical, consisting of three or four Nissen huts, in three of which the prisoners lived and slept. If there was a fourth it was used as a canteen or as a holding centre during the regular British army raids. There were two other buildings in the cage: a long hut for toilets and ablutions and a prefab Transline hut for recreation. The numbering of the Cages began at the internment end of the camp. One of the three huts in each cage was sub-divided, with half the space used for sleeping and the other half partitioned off and used as a canteen and recreation area.

Between eighty and a hundred men would be cramped in each cage, living so closely together that nothing was secret, or sacred. To break the monotony, cage-based- and even hut-based publications occasionally appeared, often penned anonymously, and consisting for the most part of 'in-house' jokes and banter, 'sleg sheets' in the same tradition as the Fron-goch papers or the original *Faoi Ghlas* which appeared in Crumlin Road in 1939-40.

In Cage 6 the *Long Kesh Hut 60 Bulletin*[169] was produced in late 1973, a four-page handwritten pamphlet, with two and three column pages and with each small article or snippet of 'news' distinguished by using different colours of pen or marker. Items in the first issue included jokes about men 'going on *Roche*' (a prescription sedative) to help in coping with the loss of liberty, and a satirical 'Warning to Junkies' to stop using *Roche* before they became addicted. Most of the small paper is given over to topical hut humour and rumour. News items included best wishes to a recently released comrade, plans for an upcoming Christmas Panto, and a short sports column:

> Last week the Sports were held in Cage 6. Taking part were competitors from the 3 huts. Great credit must be given to the organisers who did a magnificent job under the hard conditions especially Mr Owen Coogan who took full control and his assistant, Mr Gerry Adams. As was expected Hut 60 won most of the events. Pat McMahon put in a great display to win the long jump and an equally good display was given by Jeeves Butler in the high jump but the man who stole the show was Nugget Nugent taking 4 gold medals for the great Hut 60. This great athlete won the wheelbarrow race, Mr Muscles, Mr Beautiful, and a great display in the head-ducking by setting up a new record. Well done, Nugget.

The editorial, however, took a slightly more serious tone. It urged men to avoid backstabbing in the hut: 'everybody is guilty and … it can lead to fighting and bickering amongst us.' The editor also called for more attention to cleanliness and tidiness in the hut, saying that while Hut 60 'never had a reputation for being clean … this has got out of hand.' Rather than naming those responsible the editor wanted them to realise for themselves the need to keep the hut tidy 'for cage visitors and our own self-respect.'

While Long Kesh was the largest jail for male internees and sentenced prisoners, the 1970s also saw a large group of republican women being interned, and sentenced, held North and South and also

---

169   *Long Kesh Hut 60 Bulletin* (undated), Issue 1 Long Kesh: Republican Prisoners (Mark McAleese Collection).

in English prisons. The majority of women prisoners were incarcerated in Armagh Jail.

Beandando

Women prisoners in Armagh produced their own satirical paper which they named *Beandando*, an amalgamation of the titles *Beano* and *Dandy*. It was lighthearted and loaded with malicious and sometimes risqué fun, mainly at the expense of some of their imprisoned comrades. The eight-page paper was a monthly production, typed and with a hand-drawn cover. While the *Hut 60 Bulletin* editors worked incognito, the authors of *Beandando* were named in the credits at the end of each issue. Chris Clarke was the Producer, Kate McGuinness was the Editor and Margaret McClenaghan was the paper's Typist. The 'Staff' of the paper were described as 'Anonymous, and all the girls in Armagh'. Copies of *Beandando* were smuggled into Long Kesh, since much of the content was directed at internees held there, but the men don't appear to have retaliated for the verbal assaults in any of their own papers—fearing, perhaps, that the women had a lot more in their arsenal and were waiting on a chance to launch more attacks.

A light-hearted article in Issue 3, May 1974[170] titled 'Social Scene in Armagh Gaol', (written by Joan Thornbury and Marie Maguire) gave a report on the Easter concert in the prison. The cover of that edition has a sketch of Pat McClure, an internee at the time in Cage 5. The paper also carried a full-page satirical feature of what was alleged to be an internee's life history. The 'abuse' wasn't confined to their male comrades, however. Another story contained a jocular pen portrait of Angela Nelson, a fellow internee, accompanied by an equally satirical cartoon of her surrounded by sports equipment.

Other pages contained a 'Top Twenty' captioned *Top of the Pops* which had contemporary song titles matched with prisoners in both the female and male prisons; a problem page with a letter from a love-sick internee in Long Kesh and two full pages of 'scunderings'. These were short one and two-liners of often ribald teasing in the tradition of 'a little bird told me', where all of the targets of the biting humour were men in Long Kesh. No indiscretion went unnoticed! However, discretion, even fifty years later, prevents repetition or republication of some of the comments! *Beandando* made no claim to be a platform for political thought or ideology, but it played a part in providing an outlet for creativity and for relieving some of the boredom of internment in Armagh. Who knows, however, what Maeve Fitzgerald in 1918, or Bridie Connolly in 1923, would have made of the *earthy* contributions in the *Beandando!*

The first prisoners arrested and charged with specific offences in 1970 and other prisoners arrested, charged and sentenced during the following two years, were held in Crumlin Road and Armagh prisons. Despite the obvious political nature of their charges, they were denied political status or recognition in prison. All that changed when special category status was introduced in June 1972 after a hunger strike led by Billy McKee. Other prisoners in Crumlin Road joined him, as did Susan Loughran, a prisoner in Armagh. McKee, it should be remembered, had already been imprisoned in the 1930s, 1940s, 1950s and 1960s, sometimes as a sentenced prisoner, sometimes as an internee.

When the sentenced prisoners in the Crum won special category/political status they too were moved to Long Kesh shortly

---

170 *Beandando* (1974) Issue 3, May 1974 Armagh Jail: Republican Prisoners (Mark McAleese Collection).

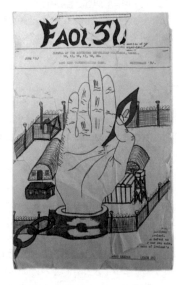

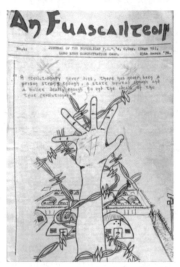

afterwards—the camp basically having been divided in two. In Long Kesh their living conditions were similar to the status granted to the internees, held at the other end of the camp. They wore their own clothes and organised their own routine. The vast majority of republican prisoners were affiliated to the mainstream Republican Movement. These prisoners in the 1970s were, as Séanna Breathnach put it years later, 'left to their own devices', ironically using the same turn of phrase Joe Cahill had used to describe life in The Crum in the 1950s.

142

In Long Kesh, 'You got your day in by studying, by walking the
yard, by running around the yard in the mornings, doing a bit of training,
by doing handicrafts, by political discussions, reading, arguing. And
basically, you were simply *left to your own devices*.'[171]

171   Séanna Breathnach: https://prisonsmemoryarchive.com/pma-for-education/life-in-the-
       cages-compounds-of-long-kesh/

Prisoners could shout across from cage to cage, but each cage, by and large, had its own regime. Some cages began producing newssheets, often a mixture of hand-produced artwork and laboriously typed columns and captions.

Some papers lasted for several issues. Individual cage newspapers appeared occasionally for short bursts of activity and sometimes the 'title' would move on with the editors if they were shifted inside the camp. In Cage 18, for example, the paper *Misneach* (*Courage*) was produced from January until at least May 1974, when Issue 10 was printed. The cover of that issue was dedicated to Volunteer Teddy Campbell who had died in the prison on 3 May 1974.

The paper *An Síoladóir* (*The Sower*) began its life in Cage 7 in May 1974 but by November of that year it was being published in Cage 10 to where the Cage 7 prisoners had been moved after 'the fire'. The Camp was relatively stable prior to 15 October 1974, but on that date the prisoners set fire to their cages, burning much of the camp to the ground in protest over deteriorating conditions and assaults.

The Burning of Long Kesh is now set in republican history as possibly the biggest battle ever between IRA Volunteers and the British Army. Hundreds of unarmed IRA prisoners fought hand-to-hand with British soldiers inside the burning prison camp and the prisoners were only subdued when CR gas canisters (a highly toxic and disabling gas the use of which remains shrouded in secrecy) was dropped from helicopters down on the POWs. In subsequent years hundreds of those prisoners have died of cancer and many questions remain to be answered about what exactly was used against them that night.[172] An internee, Hugh Coney, who attempted to escape through a tunnel below the ruins of his cage was shot dead by a British soldier.

Faoi Ghlas

In June 1974 the title *Faoi Ghlas* was in use, again, styling itself as the 'Journal of the Sentenced Republican Prisoners'. The paper appeared at irregular intervals and circulated in the cages of sentenced prisoners. Issue 4 was published in February 1976 (now sub-titled 'the Journal of Republican Prisoners of War, Long Kesh Concentration Camp'). While

172   See, for example, the Facebook activism group: CR Gas The Legacy of The Burning of Long Kesh.

the name was the same, the masthead logo was different from earlier editions, which suggests that the previous artist had either been released or transferred in the ever-changing prison population.

The hand-drawn and typewritten camp paper appears to have been published simultaneously to a typeset, folded A4-sized format, which was professionally printed and sold outside the prison. The paper printed in circulation outside used the same content as the handwritten/typed inside paper, no doubt giving its readership a unique insight into prison life and a point of contact with friends and relatives held in Long Kesh.

On the cover of Issue 4, February 1976 (on sale for six pence), the version available beyond the wire and walls had a photograph of an IRA volunteer with an RPG 7 rocket launcher at the ready. A text box below says that much of that current issue would be devoted to the British policy of *depoliticization*, 'a word Rees has introduced into the English language in his attempt to portray to the outside world all those who resist British imperialism in Ireland as "criminals".'[173] Political status had still not been removed and the use of the word 'depoliticization' is interesting in that it would quickly be exchanged for the more aggressive term, *criminalisation*. The first signs of the impending years of post-1976 protests were now showing in the prison consciousness.

The paper *Faoi Ghlas* came under criticism in an opinion piece in the national Irish language paper *Inniu* in November 1975 because of its lack of Irish language content. The author of the *Inniu* critique, Tarlach Ó hUid (at one time OC of the 1940s internees), noted that a new paper called *Faoi Ghlas* had just been started by prisoners in Long Kesh. He recalled that an earlier paper of the same name circulated among prisoners in Crumlin Road Jail in the 1940s and had been fully produced in Irish:

Bhí teorainn leis an líon cóipeanna a chuirtí i gcló' he wrote, 'toisc nach raibh ach an t-aon closcríobhán amháin ag na príosúnaigh. Toitín a luach a bhí air. Fíche cóip a chlóscríobhfaí, ceithre leathanach, agus toisc go raibh rudaí inspeise ann agus toisc gur fhag sé deis ag na príosúnaigh ar theastaigh uathu a dtuairimí a nochtadh, b'áis an-tairbheadh Faoi Ghlas sna laethanta úd.'[174]

173 *Faoi Ghlas* (1976) February 1976 No 4 Long Kesh: Republican Prisoners (P.1) Paddy Mc Menamin Collection (handwritten version) and Mark McAleese Collection (printed edition).

174 *Inniu* (1975) Samhain 1975 Dublin.

He continued, that the only thing similar about these two papers was the name, because the new paper contained no Irish. He said it was unfortunate that this was the only comparison between the 1940s prisoners and the 1970s prisoners. The 1970s prisoners, however, did not agree.

Ár nGuth Féin

Ár nGuth Féin (*Our Own Voice*) was a remarkable paper from the mid-1970s, published completely in Irish. It was the brainchild and work of Dónal Billings and a few other prisoners who could write in Irish. Because of censorship and the ban on Irish papers it took some months before *Ár nGuth Féin* had an opportunity to respond to the *Inniu* critique. In January 1976 it refuted what it considered to be unwarranted criticism:

'Le *Faoi Ghlas* sar-iriseán dá ngluaiseacht a chur i gcoimheas lenár n-iriseán nua a bhfuil an t-ainm céanna air inniu b'éigin do duine éigin bheith aineolach faoi na fiorais' wrote Dónal Mac Billings, editor of *Ár nGuth Féin*. He said that each generation of prisoners had produced Irish language papers, the name changed, but the paper contained the same drive for the language. The current *Faoi Ghlas* was in English but the paper *Ár nGuth Féin* was fulfilling the same role as *Faoi Ghlas* had in the Forties. The two current papers were both doing worthwhile work—one providing political discussion, the other carrying on with the heritage of the prison paper produced in the 1940s.

'An rud is tábhachtaí ná gur ionann linne an ghleic i gcoinne na Sasanach agus an iarracht an Ghaeilge bheith beo again ... is beo an Ghaeilge inniu i measc baill (na Gluaiseachta) ná mar a bhí sé sna 1940-50,' he wrote.[175]

Ár nGuth Féin carried articles from prisoners in different cages, linked by their zeal for the language. Brendan Curran, a prisoner in the Cages at the time recalls: 'Donal Billings was the editor, and the paper came out, I think, every two weeks for a while. It was in circulation

---

175   *Ár nGuth Féin* (1976) Uimhir 3, Eanáir 1976 Long Kesh: Republican Prisoners (Séanna Breathnach Collection).

around all the cages and was fairly popular.'[176] Brendan could not recall any disputes with the paper—'there were no libel cases … no one cared back then!'

The paper contained a mixture of typed text and hand-drawn graphics, with several copies of each issue being carefully copied down to the last detail of identical colours used in the artwork, division blocks between articles and the elaborate covers. The paper was on foolscap pages, the light card covers often made by glueing shorter lengths of card from re-cycled prison educational notebooks and exercise books and the binding was sometimes machine stitched, sometimes hand stitched and sometimes bound with homemade plastic 'staples'.

The use of Irish (or at the very least the learning of Irish) was widespread among prisoners at the time, even to the extent of some cages boasting Gaeltacht Huts, where only Irish was spoken among the prisoners. (An article in *An Eochair* in March 1977 revealed that the prisoners in the 'officials' cage were also establishing a Gaeltacht hut[177]). The number of contributors to *Ár nGuth Féin* included men from various cages. (Cages were referred to in the paper as *Cliabháin* although most prisoners still refer to the Cages as 'cásanna'.) The paper was focussed on providing a learning resource as a well as a platform for views on the struggle and each issue contained quizzes, maps of the provinces, counties and towns giving the Irish town and street names; historical and folk tales, elements of culture, sport and even 'small ads' although these were, more often than, not satirical in nature.

Among the 'oibrithe' or writers for the paper were some prisoners who would feature in the promotion of Irish in the prisons and play important roles for many years to come. Coireal Mac Curtain, for example, was very active in teaching and writing Irish in the Long Kesh Cages and a regular contributor to *Ár nGuth Féin*. After being released from Long Kesh, he was again imprisoned—in Portlaoise as a sentenced prisoner—and while there he was central to the establishment of the Gaeltacht landing. Another writer in the paper was Séanna Breathnach. In an article written a couple of months before his release in 1976 Séanna wrote of the need for community engagement and to combine political and military struggle. Before the end of that fateful year, he was back in Crumlin Road Jail, and would go on to be a leader of the H-Block/Armagh protest between 1976-81. There, he was to the forefront of teaching Irish during the blanket protest. (After his release

176 Correspondence with Brendan Curran, July 2023.
177 *Gaeltacht in Long Kesh* (1977) Long Kesh: An Eochair (No.1 March 1977) Long Kesh: Republican Prisoners (Mark McAleese Collection).

under the Good Friday Agreement he would later become a Sinn Féin elected representative on Belfast City Council.)

Other writers for the paper included Dáithí de Paor, Seán Mac Giolla Cheanna, Eoghan Ó Cougáin, Micí Ó Leanacháin, Liam Ó Cuinneagáin, Aodh Mac Chom, Seosamh Ó Maolmóire, Séamas Mac Gib, Pól Ó Gréacháin, Seán Ó Cuirín, Dáithí de Bhuídhe, Máirtín Mac Cathmhaoil agus Gearóid Ó Scolláin. Others wrote under pen names such as 'An Madra Rua' or 'An tÉireannach Neamh-Ghael', 'Na Sean Laochra', and 'Caoimhín'.

Early editions in 1976 were dominated by Frank Stagg and Gerard Mealy's hunger strike in Wakefield Prison in England (Issue 4). Frank would die a few weeks later, on 12 February that year, twenty months after the death on hunger strike of his comrade Michael Gaughan in Parkhurst Prison. Another subject of major concern were the plans to remove political status from those convicted of 'scheduled offences' after 1 March 1976. (After the summer court recess, Kieran Nugent started the blanket protest when sentenced in September 1976.)

'Beyond the wire we now have the walls of Long Kesh,' wrote the editor. 'In future these walls will hide attempts by the methods of a dictator to remove political status ... they will use terrible abuse, isolation, poor food, oppressive visits, without exercise or study or education, denying everything that reminds us we are human.'[178] Little did Dónal Mac Billing know how prescient was his depiction of the conditions that would be imposed in the as yet unfinished H-Blocks, and in Armagh Prison. That same year a booklet from the cages examining political status was written by Richard McAuley, press officer of the republican prisoners. Later, he would be Sinn Féin's Director of Publicity in the North, and northern editor of *An Phoblacht*, before becoming Gerry Adams' personal assistant during the peace process.

An Fuascailteoir

Four months after burning of the Kesh, the paper *Misneach* was replaced by *An Fuascailteoir (The Liberator),* which recognised in an editorial piece that previous cage papers often fizzled out when left to the same small group to create, contribute, and produce the paper.

---

178   *Ár nGuth Féin* (1976) Uimhir 4, Eanáir 1976 Long Kesh: Republican Prisoners (Séanna Breathnach Collection) (my translation).

An Fuascailteoir was produced in Cage 10 and had among its contributors Paddy McMcnamin, a self-taught typist and a veteran of internment on the Maidstone and Long Kesh.

'We started a Cage news sheet in 1974,' recalls Paddy McMenamin, 'and I started writing for it. I learned to type on an old black typewriter and became quite proficient ... We had a camp paper, and some cages had their own versions. They would be typed up and a few copies were made and handed round the huts.'[179] McMenamin remembered that the articles would be focussed on 'the struggle: history, education, Vietnam, Palestine ...' and like most prison newspapers there would be some 'lighter reading with a bit of slagging, sport, news, and a few cartoons.'[180]

The early issues of *An Fuascailteoir*, like *Ár nGuth Féin*, were dominated by Frank Stagg's hunger strike; while the view from the cages across the perimeter wall was of construction work progressing rapidly on the new H-Blocks.

Internment had been phased out and ended in December 1975 but the next phase of Britain's assault on the struggle—criminalisation—was just months away. To lure prisoners into conforming the British announced that those who accepted the new (H-Block) regime—and were on 'good behaviour' throughout their incarceration—would enjoy an increase in remission from one-third to one-half of their sentence. As this also had to apply to sentenced prisoners in the cages it resulted in the unexpected release of all who had passed the halfway mark in their sentence.

As political status was being removed, those still with political status in the cages would see the prison administration slowly whittling away at the rights gained after the 1972 hunger strike: their numbers dwindling and their daily lives and routine becoming ever more monotonous. Little wonder that Cage papers found it difficult to generate 'news', and instead longer political articles and analysis pieces became common. The use of Irish in the papers was mainly educational (as were the themes of the quizzes) although occasionally prose and poetry appeared *as Gaeilge*.

179 McMenamin, Paddy (2022) *From Armed Struggle to Academia*. Galway: Rivers Run Free Press (PP.102-103).

180 McMenamin, Paddy (2022) *From Armed Struggle to Academia*. Galway: Rivers Run Free Press (P.103).

The content and tone of another publishing project, in Magilligan Prison in 1975, was similar to those just described. Magilligan Camp was initially built to hold internees but by the mid-1970s it housed several hundred sentenced prisoners in cages almost identical to those in Long Kesh. The Magilligan paper was called *An Giall* (The Hostage). *An Giall* had the conventional mix of light-hearted camp banter, some Irish language content, and some serious articles too, but it was a properly-printed paper with the content smuggled out and the finished paper smuggled back into the jail on a monthly basis.

The paper was usually edited by whichever POW had been elected as the public relations officer of the prisoners. Derry's Séamus Keenan had succeeded Seosamh Ó Donnaile as editor and in time he would be followed after his release by Laurence Arbuckle. Laurence had also written for the Long Kesh Irish language paper *Ár nGuth Féin* in 1976, before his transfer to Magilligan. Both parents of Séamus Keenan, his father Seán and mother Nancy, had been interned in the 1940s and 1950s, and indeed his father had been OC of the first internees to arrive in Long Kesh in 1971, while his mother was one of nineteen women held without trial for the first half of the 1940s in Armagh Jail.

In 1975 a republican newssheet in Derry, *The Free Derry News*, began allocating a page or two each week to prisoner news, mainly from Magilligan, including extracts from *An Giall*. In August the Derry newssheet reprinted, in full, the lead article from *An Giall* which looked at whether the IRA ceasefire/truce currently in place would hold, after leading republican Daithí Ó Conaill was arrested by the Gardaí. The prisoners were under no illusion that the ceasefire was not leading to their release and warned, 'We will not be goaded into taking action by the Southern Junta (but) if the Brits fail to honour the terms of the Truce we will be faced with no alternative but to resume hostilities.'[181]

Other issues carried contributions from Armagh Jail[182] and regular coverage on behalf of a prisoner from Derry named Billy Page who, with others, was being denied Political Status.[183]

---

181 *Free Derry News* (1975) No. 4 Lúnasa 1975 Derry: Sinn Féin (Pauline Mc Cormick Collection).

182 *Free Derry News* (1975) No.5 Lúnasa 1975, Statement from Armagh POWS re. commemoration of internment anniversary) Derry: Sinn Féin (Pauline McCormick Collection).

183 Billy Page was one of a small group of prisoners sentenced to SOSP (or Detention at the Secretary of State's Pleasure), a form of life sentence for those under 18. The prison

It may be that the toughest 'editorial' which the *An Giall* editor had to write bore echoes of the *Ná Bac Leis* report of the murder of Tadhg Barry in Ballykinlar in 1921, or of the *Misneach* report of the death of Teddy Campbell in Long Kesh in 1974.

In May 1976, less than a week after being released from Magilligan Prison, Jim Gallagher was murdered by a British soldier while sitting on a bus travelling through his native city, Derry. *An Giall* tried to fathom the loss of someone who had been part and parcel of the camp's life and language just days earlier. Jim Gallagher was described as a committed Gael, and a number of issues of the paper carried articles encouraging readers to learn Irish and discussing the link between the language and political freedom.

During 1976 the prisoners wrote about the breaking down of the ceasefire in 1975, the impending political status crisis, the killing of Danny Lennon in Belfast, an ex-prisoner well known to many of those in Magilligan[184]; and articles analysing the rise of the Peace People and their failure to address British Army violence while criticising the IRA.

An Giall was in circulation in Derry and Donegal, and therefore carried some content from outside the prisons such as notices regarding support for the Prisoners' Dependants Fund, and some Sinn Féin cumainn notices. It published greetings for prisoners from family and friends (for a nominal charge of twenty pence per notice). Interestingly, one issue had several letters written not by prisoners, but by readers in London, in Sheldon, in Dublin and in Galway. Some of the articles in the paper were signed, others had pen names. One issue carried an article written by Eamonn McCann, reprinted from *Hibernia* magazine, sympathetically examining the development of the prison handicrafts

administration intended separating these younger prisoners from their comrades and planned to build a special unit in the H Block complex where they would be detained – without political status. Billy and the others began a protest in B Wing, Crumlin Road in November 1975, and were soon moved back to the Republican A Wing where various protests continued until June 1976 when they eventually won their demands and were moved to the republican cages in Magilligan Camp.

184   IRA Volunteer Danny Lennon was released on 30 April 1976 after three-and-a-half years in Long Kesh. While on active service on 10 August he was shot dead by a British soldier and the car he was driving careered out of control, and struck the Maguire family, a mother and her children on a nearby footpath. Two of the three children, Joanne and Andrew died at the scene, and the third child, John, died next day. Their mother Anne survived. The death of the children led to the formation of the Peace People. The vilification of Danny Lennon, to take the focus away from the British Army's role in the deaths; growing concerns about the torture of suspects in RUC custody; the ill-treatment of prisoners in Armagh and the H-Blocks, and hypocritical silence from the Peace People on these issues eventually led to the demise of the movement in the nationalist community by 1977.

industry through the co-operative *Siopa an Phobail*[185] in Derry, where all profits were returned to the prisoners for their welfare. The McCann article also discussed the morale of the prisoners in Magilligan, the looming battle for political status and the determination of the prisoners to resist any attempt to remove status. That battle lines were being drawn and that all the gains and conditions attached to special category status were at stake can be detected in a front page article from June 1976 reporting on denial of compassionate parole to sentenced prisoners in Magilligan.

In 1977 the prison paper was absorbed into the weekly *Republican News*—a page being reserved for prison updates—and *An Giall* ceased to exist as a separate entity. It would have ceased anyway because in January 1978 Magilligan's political prisoners were all transferred to Long Kesh.

185   Siopa an Phobail – The Peoples' Shop.

PORTLAOISE

An Trodaí

In the mid-seventies the prisoners in Portlaoise also began their own prison paper, *An Trodaí* (*The Fighter*). The paper ran from the seventies until the nineties, under the editorship at various times of Seán Mulligan, Éamonn Nolan and Liam O'Dwyer, and was produced monthly. One strategy the paper adopted was to give an equal platform to opposing sides of any proposal or policy change being advocated, as a means of informing and engaging the men on the wing as fully as possible. In 1986 when a major change in Sinn Féin strategy around abstentionism was to be debated at the Ard Fheis, for example, *An Trodaí* carried articles from comrades on the wing from both sides of the debate for many editions leading up to the Ard Fheis, and these opposing views would also be debated at the weekly Saturday-night wing meetings. When the vote eventually took place on the floor of the Ard Fheis, the Portlaoise prisoners voted along practically the same proportional lines as the delegates at the Ard Fheis had voted but no-one left the wing or walked away. *An Trodaí* had given ample opportunity to the prisoners to express their deeply-held feelings on the issue in a comradely way and the democratic vote of the membership was accepted.

'*An Trodaí* gave many young writers a platform and it overcame many obstacles over the years,' said the editors of *Portlaoise Writings,* a book of prison poetry and prose published in 1987 (edited in the jail and printed outside). It contained historical articles, book reviews, poetry and prose. Some of the contributors in time would send writings to *Listowel Writers Week*, in much the same way as prisoners in the H-Blocks would send material to *Féile an Phobail,* the West Belfast Festival.

An Trodaí was a typewritten paper with illustrations, and when each month's initial copy was made, photocopies were duplicated in the wing library to give the three landings of IRA-affiliated prisoners four or five copies each. Only one edition of *An Trodaí* was not typed. In 1985 after an escape attempt, twelve of the wing leaders were placed in solitary confinement and the typewriter was confiscated, in an uncanny repetition of the spiteful behaviour of the governor of Crumlin Road Jail in the 1940s. For that month's issue the prisoners, undaunted, produced a handwritten manuscript paper, refusing to let the system win.

Macalla (Echo)

An Trodaí was initially intended to cover the creative muse and activities of the whole wing but when the prisoners began a Gaeltacht landing in 1980-81 those prisoners realised that as the numbers on the Gaeltacht grew that they too should have a prison journal. Seosamh Ó Maoileoin remembers that, 'Prisoners in this Gaeltacht area on the top landing of Portlaoise Prison organised a wide range of activities. Among those were Irish language classes, the publication of the Irish language prison newspaper *Macalla* (*Echo*), and the organisation of Irish nights.'[186]

Nach bhFuil Aon Gaeilge Agat? An Réabhlóid

A second prison paper had the most original title of *Nach bhFuil Aon Gaeilge Agat?* (*Have ye no Irish?*). It began as a four-page paper and eventually settled on the new title of *An Réabhlóid* (*The Revolution*). This nuachtán Gaeilge was in circulation between 1983 and 1985, but the life of the paper was very much dependent on the numbers on the Gaeltacht landing, the fourth floor of the prison. As overall numbers fell, so too did the numbers in the Gaeltacht and eventually a decision was taken to amalgamate *An Réabhlóid* with *An Trodaí*. The combined paper continued with a mix of political articles, short stories, and poetry, some of which was included in *Portlaoise Writings*. It also published Irish lessons and vocabulary with occasional Irish language articles. *An Trodaí* continued publishing right into the 1990s but developments in the H-Blocks, however, were soon about to change the face of republican prison publications forever.

186 Ó Maoileoin, Seosamh (2016) in Reinisch, Dieter (2016) *Political Prisoners and the Irish Language a North South Comparison* Studi irlandesi. A Journal of Irish Studies, n. 6 (2016), pp. 239-258 DOI: http://dx.doi.org/10.13128/SIJIS-2239-3978-18464

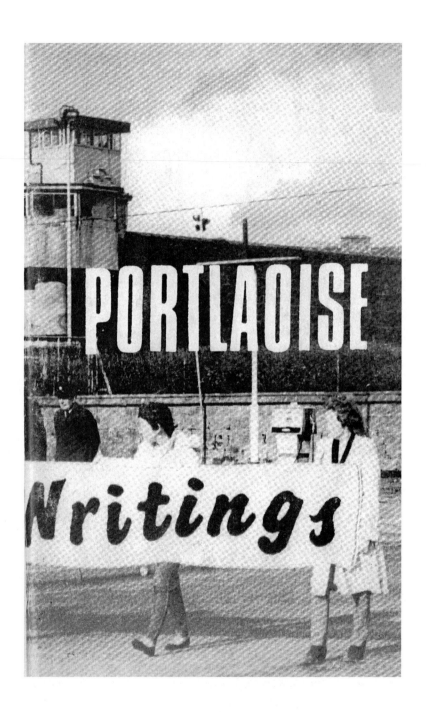

PORTLAOISE
Writings

155

H-BLOCKS, LONG KESH

Congress 86, From Long Kesh to a Socialist Republic

During the grim years of the blanket protest a few prisoners were very active in smuggling articles, poetry and publicity material out for publication in *Republican News* and later *An Phoblacht/Republican News*, the Sinn Féin paper which faithfully carried material on the prisons and prison struggles all during the protest. Foremost of these writers was, without doubt, Bobby Sands whose body of work—all written in the most stressful and difficult conditions and smuggled from the jail—included poetry, song, fiction, autobiography and satire, and his works still inspire readers to this day. Conditions did not allow for a prison paper to develop on the protest.

The years which followed the blanket protest and hunger strikes in Armagh Prison and the H-Blocks were also fraught with protests over rights and conditions in the wings. Slowly but surely, progress was made in securing educational courses. There were challenges to the unacceptable—and often bizarre—censorship restrictions. Prisoners secured a much greater degree of free association which allowed informal education, debates, and creativity to take place in the wings.

In each republican wing across the eight H-Blocks, the double-sized cells, originally designed to house 'wing orderlies', were commandeered and put to better use as wing libraries and education centres. As steadily as the ideal of the H-Blocks becoming a new University of Revolution progressed, a huge escape was being planned. Just two years after the ending of the hunger strike in which ten comrades died, thirty-eight prisoners took control of H7 and escaped. These were the very H-Blocks which the British had established, in Bobby Sands' words, as 'a breaker's yard' for republicans. The breaker's yard was now turned against the jailers. In the year after the escape, with a mixture of patience and impatience, the prisoners began fighting, again, for the type of conditions in which political education and development could flourish. Through these post-protest years, however, no H-Block 'paper' had ever evolved or appeared in print.

The unity of the prisoners so painfully achieved during the blanket protest and hunger strikes was undermined in 1986 when a small group of prisoners began acting under the banner of League of Communist Republicans. Never significant in numbers, members of the splinter group voiced discontent at the political direction of the Republican Movement. Some criticised the IRA, some criticised Sinn Féin, some criticised the prison leadership. With the help of a few like-minded people outside, a newsletter, *Congress 86*, and a booklet, *From Long Kesh to a Socialist Republic*, were produced. The titles were prison journals only in so far as prisoners provided the content. However, prison life and day-to-day news was not included in the short-lived publications which focussed more on theoretical analysis of the struggle in Ireland and world politics.

The leaders of the league eventually led their small group out of the wings in 1988, away from the conditions some of them had fought for years to achieve, to go and live in the conforming wings in Maghaberry Prison. In time, some of those who left asked to be allowed to return to the republican wings.

In 1987, in the general trend of informal education and what was being called 'awareness building', prisoners in the H-Blocks began organising poetry workshops. At first the idea of poetry was not taken too seriously but soon the idea spread from wing to wing, and block to block. From the experience gained from reading a poem aloud to the peer group, some prisoners grew confident enough to pass their writings on to local newspapers, left-wing bulletins and community-writing competitions on the outside.

Scairt Amach

It was inevitable that some internal journal would appear to collect the growing volume of prose and poetry being composed, and that publication arrived in 1987 with the first issue of *Scairt Amach* (*Shout Out*). A selection of poems written during the prison workshops were

157

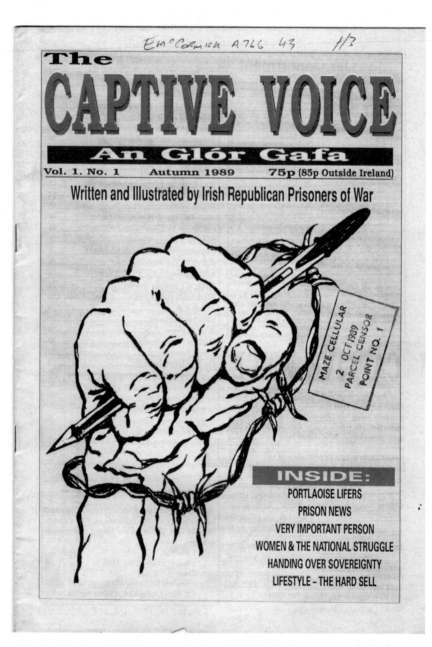

The Captive Voice / Glór Gafa. First edition, Autumn 1989

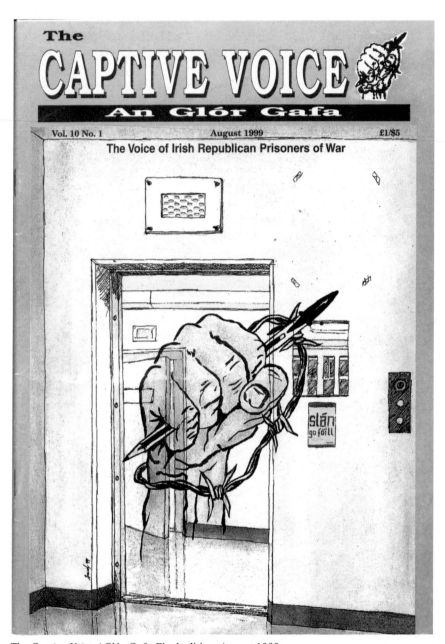

The Captive Voice / Glór Gafa. Final edition, August 1999

included in a booklet which showcased 'the best of the entries in the Creative Writing Competition in the 1989 West Belfast Festival Writing competition' and with prisoners' writing included beside writing from people outside the prison.[187]

Scairt Amach was different from previous prison papers which contained a mixture of news, political discussion, prose articles on history or analytical pieces about other conflicts alongside some poetry. *Scairt Amach* was an annual A5-sized collection of poetry only, and its editorial line was to keep encouraging its readership to write. *Scairt Amach* did not exist, however, in some literary vacuum, but was both entertainment and education, both poetic and political. No venture such as *Scairt Amach* could have occurred in the H-Blocks without the expressed approval and authority of the IRA camp leadership, since access to the scarce and limited number of typewriters, and later, word processors, was regulated and organised. *Scairt Amach* was, therefore, part of a camp strategy which drew out new skills, provided prisoners with confidence and the tools of communication while simultaneously avoiding any attempt to editorialise the actual poetry content. A poem using the metaphor of 'an old cat on a back yard wall' was as valid as some sublime verse about revolutionary consciousness in South America. Both would give encouragement to their authors, both would give the encouragement needed to take on wing, block, and camp responsibilities.

187   *The Best of the West* (1990) Belfast: West Belfast Festival. (P.1).

Iris Bheag

At the same time as *Scairt Amach* appeared, prisoners in the blocks along with republicans on the outside were attempting to develop a platform in an exclusively political journal called *Iris Bheag* (*The Little Magazine*). This A4-sized magazine, a stapled collection of discussion articles (including contributions from prisoners in the H-Blocks, Portlaoise and prisoners overseas) was edited by Jim Monaghan, head of the Sinn Féin Education Department, based at 44 Parnell Square, Dublin. The paper became, towards the end of its life, reliant on prison articles to fill its pages, while the terminology in the journal at one point drew criticism for being too marxist and at another point for the lack of contributions in Irish.

The Captive Voice/An Glór Gafa

However, for the couple of years in which *Iris Bheag* survived it was a unique and unusual collaboration between prisoners and the outside movement and stood independent and distinct from the third major publication of those years, *The Captive Voice/An Glór Gafa*. This can be seen from the editorial of *Iris Bheag*, published shortly after the first issue of *The Captive Voice* appeared: 'Some may feel that the excellent publication, *An Glór Gafa*, which has recently appeared, replaces the need for the *Iris Bheag*. This would be a mistake,' declared the editor, Jim Monaghan. 'An *Glór Gafa* is a very good publication which gives us in the movement, but also people outside, a real insight into the writing and thinking of the POWs.'

The *Iris Bheag* editor felt that the new magazine was an indication of prisoner resilience, but he said, '*Iris Bheag* serves a different purpose.' *Iris Bheag* would develop the ability to articulate and discuss ideas in a written form, and examine the course of the struggle and problems activists would face in building a political base. He wished the new magazine well: 'We certainly hope that both *An Glór Gafa* and *Iris Bheag* will continue to be forums which offer the POWs a means by which they can be part of this struggle.'[188]

Scairt Amach made no mention of the new prison publication but like *Iris Bheag* its days were numbered. The fourth edition appeared at Christmas 1990, including for the first time a poem from beyond the

188   *Iris Bheag* (1989) Nollaig 1989. Dublin: Sinn Féin Education Department (P.5).

blocks when an untitled contribution by Martina Shanahan, a republican prisoner in Durham Prison, was included. The poetry workshops were now at an end and Issue 4 reflected that conclusiveness as the pool of writers narrowed with some poets having two entries included in the final issue. In all, around 112 poems from sixty poets were published in *Scairt Amach* between 1987–1990, a record the publication could be proud of as the last copy was shared around the wings at Christmas 1990.

By that time, *An Glór Gafa* was an established magazine which, while written, edited, and designed in the prison, with writers from other prisons regularly contributing, had none of the feel of an amateur prison paper. The first issue was a 24-page, black and white edition with a spot colour of green on the cover. Marty Gough's cover illustration would become the logo of the journal in future editions, with a pen clasped in a fist with barbed wire encircling both. The main title was *The Captive Voice* but the alternative title, *An Glór Gafa*, also gained widespread usage in the prisons and beyond.

The first editor was Brian Campbell, with Leonard Ferrin as the contact person for the magazine. Over ten years the magazine would have several editors and editorial committees, usually named below the contents on the inside cover. By the end of its sixth year in 1994 the first editors had been released and the magazine was being edited by Conor Gilmore, Mícheál Mac Giolla Gunna and Paddy Devenny.

From the first issue the magazine was clearly demonstrating the oneness of all republican prisoners. Although it was edited in the H-Blocks it contained articles from Portlaoise (which continued also to publish *An Trodaí*), Maghaberry Women's Prison, republican prisoners in jails in other European countries, and even articles from Joe Doherty, a prisoner who had escaped from Crumlin Road with seven other prisoners in 1981 and who by the end of the 1980s was fighting extradition from the USA. (Doherty was also writing a prison column in *The Irish Voice*, a New York-based newspaper sympathetic to the cause of Irish freedom and which fully supported him in his battle against extradition. He would continue to write for the journal after his extradition to the H-Blocks in 1992.)

Two other points worth noting from that first issue are that the articles from Maghaberry Prison were all anonymous or in the name of 'Women POWs, Maghaberry' and that the magazine contained no Irish language articles but did contain an Irish language crossword. The absence of Irish articles in many issues was unusual given the emphasis prisoners traditionally placed on learning the language.

From the first plain, though professional issue the new journal soon appeared as a glossy covered magazine which the editor Brian Campbell and his collaborators Leonard Ferrin and Lawrence McKeown initially billed as a quarterly but which Brian would later concede was really a triannual. Early editions were out of print within weeks and the list of potential contributors for the forthcoming issues far exceeded the available space. Campbell, as editor, had to be selective and firm. *An Glór Gafa* was never a prison satire sheet: it did contain a column of humorous anecdotes poking fun at some 'off the cuff' remark or idiosyncrasy prisoners might have and display—and not confining these snippets to the blocks alone—by the all-knowing, all-seeing 'Red Spider'.[189] Most issues carried some novelties, a few poems and reviews. However, the paper often opened up debate on serious issues.

Scéalta na Sciathán

In April 1993 a group of prisoners on remand in Crumlin Road Jail brought months of planning to fruition when *Scéalta na Sciathán* was launched. Republican prisoners in the Crum were held in both A Wing and C Wing of the prison, with the two groups being kept separate. A further difficulty in communication existed because both wings also held loyalist remand prisoners. The administration's policy of integration was deliberate and unworkable. Loyalists, for example, charged with the assassination of family members of republicans were placed in adjacent cells to those very republicans and they were expected to walk the yard or sit in the same canteens together. Loyalists and republicans both demanded segregation in a protest which had been continuing since 1976. To avoid conflict, they self-segregated and used the yards and canteen alternately which meant sacrificing exercise and association time and being locked up for twice as long as they should have.

The coiste (committee) behind *Scéalta na Sciathán* believed that the arrival of the new journal would encourage political discussion, and spur on the learning of Irish and political reading among the republican remand prisoners, many of whom rightly or wrongly enviously looked on the system prevailing in the H-Blocks as being an educational nirvana.

The new journal was described in its introduction as 'an attempt at a serious magazine but there are a few light-hearted articles contained here-in.' The journal had twenty-four pages, handwritten in a prison

189   The Red Spider, a nod to the tiny insects which infested the H-Block exercise yards, was the nom de plume of the magazine's satirical columnist.

exercise book, with some illustrations. It was published over a few months and contained articles discussing the political and military situation of early 1993 and 1994, with the caveat that 'the views contained here-in may not be the views or interpretation of the Republican Movement in general.'[190]

While space in *An Glór Gafa* was available to prisoners in all of the jails, this Crumlin Road Jail journal allowed more flexibility, with more frequency for the remand prisoners to express their views in writing to each other (it was not intended for circulation beyond the jail). It gave prisoners who had already gone through the prison system, or been in the H-Blocks in earlier times, an opportunity to lead in the politicisation of their remand comrades. Kevin Lynch (Fermanagh), for example, provided a light-hearted, short ghost story in Irish but in addition gave a suggested reading list of useful republican titles and an article advocating education which echoed clearly similar sentiments included in other prison magazines, in particular an article in *Saoirse,* the Spike Island paper seventy years earlier which had appealed to prisoners not to waste the opportunity of education while interned.

'Republican POWs have always used imprisonment as an opportunity to educate ... as to what the struggle is about,' Lynch wrote, posing the rhetorical question: 'Should we allow the system to demoralize us and criminalize us or should we use the opportunity to better ourselves and our organisation?'[191] Noting that education might seem a radical change from activism outside the jail, it was 'all part of the same struggle' and that prisoners should not talk of leaving education until after being sentenced.

'We must start now!' he wrote. 'Don't put it off until the Blocks.'

Scéalta na Sciathán was a platform for poetry, polemic, politics and practical jokes, with that mix of observation of prison life, comrades' idiosyncrasies, and running through it all a sense of comradeship.

An Glór Gafa, meanwhile, as the primary journal spanning all the prisons, continued to develop and host challenging debates. One issue contained an article penned by Brendi McClenaghan discussing 'coming out', a very courageous step in prison in the early 1990s while other topics debated included the relationship between prisoners and their partners on the outside; relationships between prisoners and their

190 Scéalta na Sciathán (1993) No.1 (https://tinyurl.com/bdz65xr9) No.1, P.2 (with permission from Mící Ceinnseallaigh).

191 *Scéalta na Sciathán* (1993) No.1 (https://tinyurl.com/bdz65xr9) No.1, P.7 (with permission from Mící Ceinnseallaigh).

children. As the peace process of the mid-1990s gathered pace, *An Glór Gafa* published views and comments and the prisoners' own submission to the process. Much of this was, of course, aimed at an audience outside the walls which was just as important to the writers as their readership inside the walls. No other prison writings since the time of Liam Mellow's *Notes from Mountjoy* were scrutinised so closely in real-time as were the columns of *An Glór Gafa*.

The years had emboldened the prisoners to throw down the gauntlet at the censors. The 'copy' for each edition of the unique paper was sent out via the prison censor in an act of defiance, and refusal to compromise on the prisoners' beliefs. (Bets were, of course, hedged, with a secure duplicate copy being smuggled out for each issue, in the event that the censor would block some offending article.) The magazine in time was as important a weathervane for republican thinking as the weekly *An Phoblacht/Republican News* or the annual *IRIS* magazine.

BOOKS

In spite of many obstacles, searches and censorship, booklets and even full-length books were also produced from within the prisons, particularly in the 1970s—1990s. Reference has already been made to Mellows' *Notes from Mountjoy*, published posthumously. But it was in 1975 that a complete book of prison writings appeared. The attention grabbling title of *Have You No Anger?*[192] appeared as some men in Long Kesh turned their hands to poetry. The editor was Derek Thompson and the book was published for the prisoners by Clann na nGaedheal in Dublin. The introduction declared that 'This collection of poems was put together between early morning raids by the British Army and weekly searches by prisoner officers. Its very existence is our answer to the futile attempts of the establishment to harass, torture and suppress us'.[193]

Containing thirty-two poems, almost twenty prisoners contributed to the collection of verse which looked at politics, fallen comrades, prison conditions and struggle. Some of the poets were also, as might be expected, contributors to the prison newspapers circulating at the time and at least one poet, Robbie Lavery, would again feature years later while serving another sentence, in issues of *Scairt Amach,* a poetry collection published in the H-Blocks.

In 1975—with the establishment of the Republican Press Centre in Belfast in 1973—some individual prisoners' writings began to appear in booklet form. In September 1976 a seminal booklet penned by Gerry Adams, *Peace in Ireland*,[194] began discussing for the first time the path towards an end to the conflict. Gerry Adams was by that time a sentenced prisoner in Cage 11 in Long Kesh. He had begun writing in the *Republican News* in 1975 (some of the articles would be published in the collection *Cage 11* in 1990). Other prisoners, including Bobby Sands, were also putting pen to paper at the time while artists like Danny Devenny (who illustrated Adams' booklet) were cutting their creative teeth.

---

192 Republican Prisoners, Long Kesh (1975) *Have you No Anger?* Dublin: Clann na nGaedheal.

193 Republican Prisoners, Long Kesh (1975) *Have you No Anger?* Dublin: Clann na nGaedheal (foreword).

194 Adams, Gerry (1976) *Peace in Ireland.* Belfast: The Republican Press Centre.

The sixteen-page booklet described as written by 'Gerry Adams, Faoi Ghlas ag Gallaibh', was dedicated to: 'Danny Lennon, who died for peace, and for the Maguire children who were killed with him.' (See footnote 183). Danny was an IRA Volunteer, shot by the British Army, who just a few months earlier had been walking the same prison cage yard as Adams. A cypher on the cover design incorporates the words: 'Dan, Dee, Paddy and Me', with Adams referring to his cage comrades, Danny Devenny, Dee Delaney (who was killed in action shortly after his release), Paddy Molloy, editor of the Cage paper *An Giolla*, and Adams, himself. The small booklet would, in time, help seed our Peace Process.

Later the same year Republican Publications produced *In the Care of Her Majesty's Prisons*[195] by Hugh Feeney, a prisoner who had spent over 200 days on hunger strike and being force-fed (along with Gerry Kelly and Dolours and Marion Price) in Brixton Prison in 1973-74, demanding transfer to a jail in the North of Ireland. Feeney's booklet was dedicated to the memory of hunger strikers Michael Gaughan and Frank Stagg who died in 1974 and 1976 respectively; Noel Jenkinson, a prisoner who died of medical neglect in an English prison in October 1976; and to Máire Drumm, herself an ex-prisoner, murdered in her hospital bed, also in October 1976. Hugh Feeney would continue his prison writing career, contributing to *Republican News* under different pen-names during the remainder of his imprisonment.

The ground-breaking *Prison Struggle: The story of Continuing Resistance Behind the Wire* was published by the Republican Press Centre in 1977. The 64-page book was composed in the cages of Long Kesh and contained a range of articles, written by different prisoners describing life in the prison. Smuggled cameras allowed a view of the reality of life behind the wire, while sketches added to the clandestine nature of the publication. None of the authors are named although some of the artwork, at least, was created by Danny Devenny, including a line-map of the prison layout showing an as yet unexplored extension to the prison camp known simply as 'H-Block'. The compilation appears to have been written during 1975 and early 1976 and sections of the book were already out of date by the time of its publication. The description of conditions in A Wing, Crumlin Road, for example, were based on a life with political status, but by 1977 the blanket protest had already begun.

195 Feeney, Hugh (1976) *In the Care of Her Majesty's Prisons.* Belfast: The Republican Press Centre.

Themes covered in the chapters of the book include: Remand; The Courts; First Impressions (of the Cages); Screws; Education; An Ghaeilge. The latter article in Irish, discussing the use of Irish in the Cages and the beginning of Gaeltacht Huts, is thought to have been written by Bobby Sands before his release from the Cages in 1976. Chapters on Prisoners' Aid and Activities recount the production of handicrafts, sports days, and concerts.

A chapter titled Medical Facilities recalled the death of IRA Volunteer Jim Moyne, a Derry internee who died of medical neglect in 1975. A chapter on Escapes gave a sense of the claustrophobic conditions in a tunnel, and included was a photograph of a tunnel being excavated. There were also chapters on The H-Blocks and on Prisoner of War Status. The book provided a view of life in Long Kesh which was more detailed and insightful than any earlier publication.

In 1980 the Sinn Féin POW Department in Dublin published *Special Category A*[196], an account written by John Higgins, a prisoner in England describing the conditions in which Irish prisoners were held. Seven years later a posthumous account of life in prison in Britain *Inside an English Jail*[197] by IRA Volunteer Raymond McLaughlin would provide more detail, and add to the corpus of Irish prison biography, stretching back through Clarke, Davitt and Rossa to Mitchel.

Meanwhile, Bobby Sands' writing career continued in the H-Blocks. Bobby, during his earlier incarceration in the Cages, had also been writing for the Cage 11 paper *An Giolla*. On his arrival in the H-Blocks in 1977 he was appointed PRO and took on the Herculean task of breaking through the censorship and powerful propaganda machine which the British Government had created in the battle to criminalise republican prisoners. He wrote comms and songs, poetry, prose, and press-statements, furiously filling his days with the same 'fever of war' described by Peadar O'Donnell as filling prison writings in Mountjoy sixty years earlier.

Others, too, were writing. *The Crunch Has Come*[198] was a book written on toilet paper and smuggled from the H-Blocks in 1980. It told in grim detail of the life on the protest. Written under a pseudonym, Frankie O'Brien, the 56-page book gave a first-hand account of life on one of the protest wings, in raw, unedited language. It was published in March 1981, just as the second hunger strike began. The book, like most

196 Higgins, John (1980) *Special Category A*. Dublin: Sinn Fein POW Department.
197 McLaughlin, Raymond (1987) *Life in an English Jail*. Dublin: Borderline Publications.
198 O'Brien, Frankie (pseudonym of Mac Cormaic, Eoghan) (1981) *The Crunch Has Come*. Baltimore USA: Boulevard Offset Company.

republican publications, was banned by the prison censor and NIO Prisons' Department on the grounds that 'it contains thinly disguised references to prison officers'.

In April of that fateful year *The Writings of Bobby Sands*[199] was published, a 36-page booklet, introduced by Gerry Adams, with selected articles previously published in *Republican News* (and *An Phoblacht/Republican News* after the papers merged in 1979). It would be the first of many publications gleaned from the huge body of prison writings from Bobby's pen, published after his death.

In May 1981, in the wake of Bobby's death, a twelve-page booklet by Ruairí Ó Dónaill, based on the account of Noel Ó Casaide, a recently-released blanket man from Monaghan, was produced by the National H Block/Armagh Committee. *Seachtain ar an Bhlaincéad*[200] was published in Irish, recognising that Irish by that time was widely spoken in the H-Blocks.

In June 1981 *The Diary of Bobby Sands*[201] with an introduction by Danny Morrison was published. In October, after the hunger strike ended with the death of Bobby and nine of his comrades, his book *Prison Poems* was published. A substantial collection of over eighty pages, once again introduced by Danny Morrison, the book contained the epic twenty-page trilogy, *The Crime of Castlereagh*. Two years after Bobby's death, the much larger work, the semi-autobiographical memoir of the blanket protest, *One Day in My Life*[202] came out. Bobby Sands' works have never been out of print in all the years since then.

The protest in Armagh Prison was also recounted, first hand, by the writer Margaretta D'Arcy in her 1981 book *Tell Them Everything*. Fined for staging a protest against the conditions in Armagh Prison on International Womens' Day in 1979, D'Arcy refused to pay the fine and spent three months on the protest wing of the jail. While often in an awkward 'fit' with the ideology of the women on protest, Margaretta D'Arcy's book did raise 'crucial questions for the women's movement: can it remain silent in face of the suffering and resistance of the republican women prisoners.'[203]

199   Sands, Bobby (1981) *The Writings of Bobby Sands*. Dublin: Sinn Féin POW Department.
200   Ó Casaide, Noel & Ó Dónaill, Ruairí (1981) *Seachtain ar an Bhlaincéad*. Dublin: Coisde Náisiúnta H-Blocanna/Ard Mhacha.
201   Sands, Bobby (1981) *The Diary of Bobby Sands*. Dublin: Sinn Féin Publicity Department.
202   Sands, Bobby (1983) One Day in My Life, Cork: The Mercier Press.
203   D'Arcy, Margaretta (1981) *Tell Them Everything* London: Pluto Press (cover comment).

In the 1980s other publications would appear, sometimes as individual works, other times as collective works. In July 1987 prisoners in Portlaoise produced a collection. *Portlaoise Writings*[204] contained prose and poetry and was a bi-lingual publication encompassing a selection of writings from a decade and a half of imprisonment in that jail. 1988 also saw the publication of *Fite Fuaite*[205], a book of Irish language crosswords compiled in the prison (and a second volume, *Lúb ar Lár*[206] appeared in 1989) as some prisoners immersed themselves in the Irish language. This was also reflected in the Sinn Féin publication *The Role of the Language in Ireland's Cultural Revival*[207], published in 1986. In 1991 a twenty-page booklet, *Éirí na Gealaí: Reflections on the Culture of Resistance in Long Kesh*[208], was published and contained contributions from four current, and one recently released H-Block prisoner. The booklet was described as 'scríbhinní Chimí na Ceise Fada' and various chapters discussed the history of 'Irish On the Blanket' by Peadar Whelan; 'The Culture of Republican Wings' by the booklet's editor; 'Prison Publications' by Brian Campbell, editor of *The Captive Voice;* 'Séanadh Ceart Cultúrtha sa Jailtacht' by Mac Cormaic and a foreword by former prisoner, Marcas Mac Ruairí.

Gerry Kelly, who had been on the long hunger strike of 1974 and who had escaped from the H-Blocks in 1983, was recaptured in Holland in 1986 and extradited back to the North. He was released in 1989, the same year he published his first collection of poetry, *Words from a Cell*[209]. In later years he would publish a definitive account of the Great Escape, as well as other books of memoirs and poetry.

In 1991 the book *H-Block, A Selection of Poetry by Republican Prisoners* was published by a writers' group in England. Some contacts had been built up and as poems were submitted, the South Yorkshire Writers' Group agreed to publish a selection of work. The West Belfast Festival were also happy to produce a book of poetry, *The Best of the West,* which included writers inside, and outside the prisons. During these years Danny Morrison, who had been the lead figure in republican publicity and curator of much of Bobby's writings was himself

204   Republican Prisoners (1987) *Portlaoise Writings.* Dublin: Republican Publications.
205   Mac Cormaic, Eoghan (1988) *Fite Fuaite.* Belfast: Nuacht.
206   Mac Cormaic, Eoghan (1989) *Lúb ar Lár.* Belfast: Nuacht.
207   *The Role of the Language in Ireland's Cultural Revival* (1986) Belfast: Sinn Féin Culture Department.
208   Republican Prisoners (ed. O'Hagan, Felim) (1991) *Éirí na Gealaí: Reflections on the Culture of Resistance in Long Kesh.* Belfast: Roinn an Chultúir Shinn Féin.
209   Kelly, Gerry (1989) *Words From a Cell.* Belfast: Sinn Féin Publications.

imprisoned. He continued to write while in prison, including a weekly column, 'Radio Times' for *An Phoblacht/Republican News*, and for *The Captive Voice* as a contributor and book reviewer.

His second novel, *On the Back of the Swallow*, written while in the H-Blocks, was published nine months before his release in 1995. He had also begun work on another novel, *The Wrong Man*, and this was completed and published two years later.

The Captive Voice/An Glór Gafa continued to spark other prison writing and in the early nineties a music 'cassette', taped secretly inside a H-Block was issued and a full volume of H-Block writings was produced. This unique and insightful history of the H-Block/Armagh struggle and hunger strike, *Nor Meekly Serve My Time*, was published while almost all the contributors were still imprisoned. The book is now in its third edition. Some prisoners who began scribbling for the early editions of *An Glór Gafa* continued to write long years after.

The prisoners' own Education Department, in conjunction with the Sinn Féin Education Department, produced a book, *Questions of History*, which became required reading for the prison education program. Brian Campbell, the first editor of *An Glór Gafa,* went on to edit *An Phoblacht Republican News;* Laurence McKeown became an established writer and playwright, as did others who put pen to paper for the journal over the decade of the 1990s.

The final edition of *An Glór Gafa* broke with tradition. The journal was coming to an end as the last of the prisoners were being released in July 2000 and the editors invited Lawrence McKeown to write the final editorial for what had become one of the the longest running, most widely read, and most wide ranging of any republican prison publication.

In the first editorial in 1989 Brian Campbell had written:

'We are political prisoners in every sense of the term. In gaol we continue as political activists determined to do all in our power to bring about the day when British troops no longer walk our streets and imperialism's writ no longer runs in our country. *An Glór Gafa* will reflect this by presenting our views on those issues which affect the daily lives of people throughout Ireland and by suggesting our ideas for a way forward. It will also bring to life our feelings and experiences through poetry and short stories. We hope our Captive Voice will be heard by all those who share our vision of freedom in a socialist Republic'.[210]

Now, in an act of completion, Laurence brought the historic publication to a close:

'In other circumstances it would be sad to see such an exciting, innovative publication come to an end but if it signals the release of all republican prisoners then it is to be welcomed. Let's hope though that the creative talents and radical voices that came together to make *An Glór Gafa* the success that it was, continue to find expression on the outside. Our voices may no longer be held in captivity but that doesn't mean that they are totally free. Beirigí bua uilig.'[211]

Finally, in 2000 the H-Blocks closed. Maghaberry and Portlaoise prisoners were released under the Good Friday Agreement and *An Glór Gafa* joined the long list of titles to have carried the prisoners' stories and voices in captivity. The final cover presented an eerie echo of the first cover, which had a hand clutching a pen and circled by barbed wire. Now, the hand and pen faded over prison cell doors lying open, empty, with the prison cell-cards bearing the legend 'Slán go foill'. Perhaps 'Slán *go deo*' might have been more properly what was in the artist's mind.

210   *The Captive Voice/ An Glór Gafa* (1989) Long Kesh: Republican Publications (Vol.1. No.1 Autumn, 1989).
211   *The Captive Voice/ An Glór Gafa* (1989) Long Kesh: Republican Publications (Vol.10. No.1 August, 1999).

APPENDIX

A chronology of prison journals and newspapers created by republican prisoners between 1865 and 2000.

Fenian pin-pricked news sheets on toilet paper – in Pentonville Prison 1865

News written on tongues of prison boots – in Portland Prison 1866

The Wild Goose – on the prison ship Hougoumont in the 1867

Untitled newspaper style notes and bulletins between Daly and Clarke - Chatham Prison 1880s

The Irish Felon – in Chatham Prison in the 1880s

The Daily Rumour – in Frongoch in 1916

The Daily Wire – in Frongoch in 1916

The Frongoch Favourite – in Frongoch in 1916

An Foraire/The Outpost – in Reading Jail in 1916

An Bhuabhall – in Lewes Prison in 1916

The Truth: A journal of uncommon sense – Dundalk Jail in 1918

Glór na Carcrach – in Crumlin Road Jail in 1918

The JailBirds Journal – in Crumlin Road Jail in 1918

The Insect – in Lincoln Prison in 1918

Louis Walshes circulars – in Derry Jail in 1920

Ná Bac Leis – in Ballykinlar in 1920

The Barbed Wire – in Ballykinlar in 1920

Faoi Ghlas – in Crumlin Road Jail 1920-21

Saoirse – in Spike Island in 1921

The Book of Cells – in Mountjoy in 1922

The Sniper – in Mountjoy in 1922

The Trumpeter – in Mountjoy in 1922

The Ship's Bulletin – on the Argenta in 1923

C Weed – in Mountjoy in 1923

An Barr Buaidh – in Mountjoy in 1923
NDU Invincible – in the North Dublin Union in 1923
Poblacht na hÉireann/An Phoblacht – in Newbridge Camp in 1923
The Tintown Herald – possibly in The Curragh in 1923-24
Faoi Ghlas (in English) – in Crumlin Road Jail in 1940
Journal produced by Séamus Ó Goilidhe - in Arbour Hill in 1940
Faoi Ghlas (in Irish) – in Crumlin Road Jail in 1941-42
An Drithleog – in Derry Jail in 1942
An Fréamh – in Derry Jail in 1943
An Chúis – in Derry Jail in 1943
Faoi Ghlas – in Crumlin Road Jail in 1944-45
An Coimhéadóir – in Crumlin Road Jail in 1944-45
Unnamed paper, possibly *The Bell* – Mountjoy Prison 1940s
Splanc – in The Curragh in 1940-44
Barbed Wire – in The Curragh in 1940-44
An Braighdeán – in Crumlin Road Jail in 1958
The Sinn Féiner – in Crumlin Road Jail in 1959
An Timire – in Crumlin Road Jail in 1959
Saoirse – in Crumlin Road Jail in 1961
Barbed Wire Bulletin – in Long Kesh in 1972
Drithleog – prisoners' news compiled in Long Kesh, published in USA 1971-73
Hut 60 Bulletin – in Long Kesh in 1972
An Eochair – in Long Kesh in 1973
Ár nGuth Féin – in Long Kesh in 1974
Faoi Ghlas – in Long Kesh in 1974
Misneach – in Long Kesh in 1974
An Síoladóir – in Long Kesh in 1974
An Fuascailteoir – Long Kesh in 1974
An Giall – in Magilligan in 1974
Beandando – in Armagh Jail in 1974
An Giolla – in Long Kesh (Cage 11) 1976
An Trodaí – in Portlaoise Prison in the 1970s-90s
Macalla – in Portlaoise Prison in 1980
Nach bhFuil Aon Ghaeilge agat? – in Portlaoise Prison in the 1980s
An Réabhlóid – in Portlaoise Prison in the 1980s
Congress 86 – compiled in H Blocks, printed outside.

From Long Kesh to a Socialist Republic– compiled in H
Blocks, printed outside.
Scairt Amach – in the H-Blocks in 1987-90
Iris Bheag – in the H-Blocks and outside the prisons in 1987-
90
Scéalta na Sciathán – in Crumlin Road Jail 1993
An Glór Gafa/the Captive Voice – H-Blocks and various
prisons 1989-2000

BIBLIOGRAPHY
(including books not referenced in the text)

Adams, Gerry (1976) *Peace in Ireland.* Belfast: The Belfast
  Republican Press Centre
Adams, Gerry (1990) *Cage Eleven.* Tralee: Brandon
Adams, Gerry & McAuley, Richard (2002) *The Armagh
  Women.* Belfast: An Fhuiseog
Ambrose, Joe (2008) *The Fenian Anthology.* Cork: Mercier
  Press
Anderson, Brendan (2015) *Joe Cahill, A Life in the IRA.*
  Dublin: The O'Brien Press
Andrews, CS (2001) *Dublin Made Me.* Dublin: Lilliput Press
Behan, Brendan (1958) *Borstal Boy.* London: Corgi
Behan, Brendan (1990) *Confessions of an Irish Rebel.* London:
  Arrow Books
Boyce, Eamonn (undated) *Random Thoughts and Reminisces.*
  Dublin: unpublished
Brady, Evelyn (2011) *In the Footsteps of Anne.* Belfast:
  Shanway
Breathnach, Diarmuid & Ní Mhurchú, Máire (1990)
  Beathaisnéis a Dó, Dublin: An Clóchomhar Tta
Brennan-Whitmore, WJ (2013) *With the Irish in Frongoch.*
  Cork: Mercier Press
Bryson, Anna (2008) *The Insider: The Belfast Prison Diaries
  of Eamonn Boyce, 1956–1962.* Dublin: Lilliput Press
Buckley, Margaret (2022) *The Jangle of the Keys.* Dublin: Sinn
  Féin
Campbell, Joseph (2001) (Ed. Ní Chuilleanáin, Eiléan) *As I
  Was Among The Captives.* Cork: Cork University Press
Carey, Tim (2000) *Mountjoy. The Story of a Prison.* Dublin:
  The Collins Press

Carroll-Burke, Peter (2000) *Colonial Discipline, The Making of the Irish Convict System*. Dublin: Four Courts Press

Casey, John Sarsfield (2005) *The Galtee Boy*. Dublin: University College Dublin Press

Cashman, Denis B (2001) (Ed. Sullivan III, CW) *Fenian Diary* Dublin: Wolfhound Press

Clarke, Kathleen (1991) *Revolutionary Woman*. Dublin: The O'Brien Press

Clarke, Thomas J. (1922) *Glimpses of an Irish Felon's Prison Life*. Dublin: Maunsell and Roberts

Comerford, Máire (2021) *On Dangerous Ground: A Memoir of the Irish Revolution*. Dublin: Lilliput Press

Coogan, Tim Pat (1980) *On the Blanket. The H-Block Story*. Dublin: Ward River Press

Coogan, Tim Pat (1980) *The IRA*. Glasgow: Fontana

D'Arcy, Margaretta (1981) *Tell Them Everything*. London: Pluto Press

D83222 (anon.), Preface by Seán Ó Faoláin (1945) *I Did Penal Servitude*. Dublin: Metropolitan Publishing

Darragh, Síle (2011) *John Lennon's Dead*. Belfast: Beyond the Pale (repub. 2022)

de Blaghd, Éarnán (1973) *Gaeil á Múscailt*. Dublin: Sáirséal agus Dill

Devlin, Anne (1968) (Ed. Finegan, John) *The Prison Journal of Anne Devlin*. Cork: Mercier

Devlin, Bernadette, (1969) *The Price of My Soul*. London: Pan

Devlin, Bobby (1985) *An Interlude with Seagulls*. London: Information on Ireland Publications

Devlin, Paddy (1983) *Straight Left*. Belfast: Blackstaff Press

Donnelly, Dónal (2010) *Prisoner 1082*. Dublin: Collins Press

Douglas, Robert (2008) *At Her Majesty's Pleasure*. London: Hodder

Dunne, Declan (2012) *Peter's Key*. Cork: Mercier Press

Durney, James (2019) *Interned*. Cork: Mercier Press

Ebenezer, Lyn (2006) *Fron-goch*. Wales: Gwasg Carreg Gwalch

English, Richard & O'Malley, Cormac (1991) *Prisoners. The Civil War Letters of Ernie O'Malley*. Dublin: Poolbeg

Fallon, Charlotte H (1986) *Soul of Fire: A biography of Mary MacSwiney*. Cork: Mercier

Figgis, Darrell (1917) *A Chronicle of Cells.* Dublin: Talbot Press

Gallagher, Frank (1967) *Days of Fear.* Cork: Mercier Press

Greg, Patrick (2007) *The Crum.* Dublin: Gill & McMillen

Grew, BD (Major) (1958) *Prison Governor.* London: Herbert Jenkins

Harvey, Dan (2016) *Soldiers of the Short Grass.* Kildare: Merrion

Henderson, Frank (1998) *Frank Henderson's Easter Rising. Recollections of a Dublin Volunteer.* Cork: Cork University Press

Higgins, John (1980) *Special Category A.* Dublin: Sinn Féin POW Department.

Hogan, David (*nom de plume* for Frank Gallagher) (1953) *The Four Glorious Years.* Dublin: Irish Press Limited

Howard, Paul (1996) *The Joy.* Dublin: The O'Brien Press

Kearney, Seamus (2021) *No Greater Love.* Belfast

Kearns, Linda (1922) *In Times of Peril, Easter 1916— Mountjoy 1921.* Dublin: Talbot Press

Kelly, Gerry (1989) *Words From a Cell.* Belfast: Sinn Féin Publications

Kelly, Gerry (2013) *The Escape.* Belfast: M&G Publications

Kelly, Gerry (2021) *Inside Out.* Belfast

Kleinrichert, Denise (2001) *Argenta 1922.* Kildare: Irish Academic Press

Leabhar na hArd-Fheise, Chonradh na Gaeilge (1980) (https://issuu.com/cnag/docs/1980af)

Leabhar na hArdFheise, Chonradh na Gaeilge (1982) (https://issuu.com/cnag/docs/1982af)

Lonergan, John (2010) *The Governor.* London: Penguin Books

Macardle, Dorothy (1968) *The Irish Republic.* London: Corgi

MacBride, Maud Gonne (1995) *A Servant of the Queen.* Dublin: Golden Eagle Books

MacBride, Seán (2005) *That Day's Struggle, Memoir 1904– 1951.* Dublin: Currach Press

MacCormaic, Alison (2016, MA Thesis, unpublished) *Prison Handicrafts among Republican Prisoners, 1916–2000.* Dublin: NCAD

MacCurtain, Fionnuala (2003) *Remember ... It's for Ireland.* Cork: Mercier History

MacIonnrachtaigh, Feargal (2013) *Language, Resistance and Revival*. London: Pluto Press

MacEoin, Uinseann (1997) *The IRA in the Twilight Years 1923–1948*. Dublin: Argenta Publications

Mac Siacais, Jake (2020) *On Taobh Istigh*. Dublin: Coiscéim

Markievicz, Countess (1987) *Prison Letters of Countess Markievicz*. London: Virago

Maskey, Seán (2011) *Long Kesh–My Lost Freedom*. Belfast: Shanway Press

Matthews, Anne (2012) *Dissidents*. Dublin: Mercier Press

McCafferty, Nell (1981) *The Armagh Women*. Dublin: Co-Op Books

McCann, Jim (1999) *The Gates Flew Open*. Belfast: Glandore Publishing

McCann, Jim (1999) *Growing Up in Long Kesh*. Belfast: Glandore Publishing

McCann, Jim (Jaz) (2020) *6000 Days*. Germany: Elsinor Verlag

McCarron, Frankie (2005) *Magilligan POW Memories*. Derry

McCauley, Chrissie (1989) *Women in a War Zone*. Belfast: Republican Publications

McConville, Seán (1981) *A History of English Prison Administration, Vol 1, 1750–1877*. London: Routledge & Kegan Paul

McConville, Seán (2021) *Irish Political Prisoners 1960–2000, Braiding Rage and Sorrow*. London: Routledge

McCoole, Sinéad (2000) *Guns and Chiffon*. Dublin: The Stationary Office

McCoole, Sinéad (2003) *No Ordinary Women*. Dublin: The O'Brien Press

McGlinchey, Paul (2021) *Truth Will Out*. Bellaghy

McGuffin, John (1973) *Internment*. Tralee: Anvil Books

McGuffin, John (1974) *The Guinea Pigs*. Middlesex: Penguin

McKeown, Laurence (2001) *Out of Time*. Belfast: Beyond the Pale Publications

McKeown, Laurence (2021) *Time Shadows*. Belfast: Beyond the Pale Publications

McLaughlin, Raymond (1987) *Inside an English Jail*. Ireland: Borderline Publications

McMenamin, Paddy (2022) *From Armed Struggle to Academia*. Galway: Rivers Run Free Press

Mitchel, John (1983) *Jail Journal*. London: Sphere

Monaghan, Jim (2007) *Colombia Jail Journal*. Kerry: Mount Eagle Publications

Morrison, Danny (1997) *Then the Walls Came Down: A Prison Journal*. Cork: Mercier Press

Murray, Raymond (1998) *Hard Time*. Cork: Mercier Press

Nic Cormaic, Eibhlín (2022, unpublished) *Feminism and Irish among Women Republican Prisoners 1970–2000*. Belfast: QUB

Nic Giolla Easpaig, Áine agus Eibhlín (1986) *Girseacha i nGéibheann*. Westport: FNT

Nic Giolla Easpaig, Áine agus Eibhlín (1987) *Sisters in Cells*. Westport: FNT

Ó Briain, Liam (1951) *Cuimhní Cinn*. Dublin: Sáirseal agus Dill

Ó Cadhain, Máirtín (1973) *As an nGéibheann*. Dublin: Sáirséal agus Dill

Ó Cathasaigh, Aindrias (2002) *Ag Samhlú Troda: Máirtín Ó Cadhain 1905–1970*. Baile Átha Cliath: Coiscéim

Ó Cathasaigh, Aindrias (2016) *Athrú ag Teacht*. Baile Átha Cliath: Coiscéim

Ó Cléirigh, Nellie (2003) *Hardship and High Living, Irish Women's Lives 1808–1923*. Dublin: Portobello Press

Ó Dochartaigh, Tomás (1969) *Cathal Brugha, a shaol is a thréithe*. Dublin: FNT

Ó Dónaill, Ruairí & Casaide, Noel (1981) *Seachtain ar an Bhlaincéad*. Dublin: Coiste Náisiúnta H-Blocanna/Ard Mhacha

Ó Donnabháin Rossa, Diarmuid (1991) *Irish Rebels in English Prisons*. Tralee: Brandon

Ó Donnabháin Rossa, Diarmuid (2004) *Rossa's Recollections 1838-98*. Maryland, USA: Rowman & Littlefield

Ó Duibhginn, Seosamh (1962) *Ag Scaoileadh Sceoil*. Baile Átha Cliath: An Clóchomhar Tta.

Ó Duibhir, Liam (2013) *Prisoners of War, Ballykinlar Internment Camp 1920–21*. Cork: Mercier

Ó Gaora, Colm (1969) *Mise*. Dublin: Oifig an tSólathair

Ó hUid, Tarlach (1985) *Faoi Ghlas*. Dublin: FNT

Ó Maoileoin, Séamas (1958) *B'fhiú an Braon Fola*. Dublin: Sáirseal agus Dill

Ó Muireadhaigh, Liam P. (1946) *Some Reminiscences of Tough Times.* Belfast: unpublished manuscript
Ó Suilleabháin Diarmaid (1983) *Ciontach.* Dublin: Coiscéim
Ó Tuama, Seán (Ed.) (1993) *The Gaelic League Idea.* Cork: Mercier
Ó Tuathaigh, Gearóid (Eag.) (2016) *An Piarsach Agus 1916.* Galway: Cló Iar-Chonnacht
O'Brien, Frankie (Mac Cormaic, Eoghan) (1981) *The Crunch Has Come.* Baltimore, USA: Boulevard Offset Co
O'Donnell, Peadar (2013) *The Gates Flew Open.* Cork: Mercier
O'Donoghue, Florence (1971) *The Complete Book of IRA Jailbreaks 1918–21.* Dublin: Anvil Books
O'Driscoll, Seán (2022) *Heiress, Rebel, Vigilante, Bomber: The Extraordinary Life of Rose Dugdale.* Dublin: Penguin
O'Farrell, Padraic (1997) *Who's Who in the War of Independence and Civil War.* Dublin: Lilliput Press
O'Hagan, Des (2012) *Letters from Long Kesh.* Dublin: Citizen Press
O'Hara, Tony (2021) *The Time Has Come.* Derry
O'Hare, Rita *Rita.* (Expected date of publication, May 2024)
O'Mahony, Sean (1987) *Frongoch.* Dublin: FDR Teoranta
O'Malley, Ernie (2012) *On Another Man's Wound.* Cork: Mercier Press
O'Malley, Ernie (2002) *The Singing Flame.* Trá Lí: Anvil
O'Neill, Tom (2021) *Spike Island's Republican Prisoners, 1921.* Cheltenham: The History Press
O'Sullivan, Michael (1999) *Brendan Behan: A Life.* Dublin: Blackwater Press
O'Sullivan, Ted (2022) *Bere Island Internment Camp, 1921. Nora O'Neill's Autograph Book.*
Priestly, Philip (1999) *Victorian Prison Lives.* London: Pimlico
Republican Prisoners (1987) *Portlaoise Writings.* Dublin: Republican Publications
Republican Prisoners (2015) *Their Prisons, Our Stories.* Clones: Fáilte Cluain Eois
Republican Prisoners (Eag. O'Hagan, F) (1991) *Éirí na Gealaí: Reflections on the Culture of Resistance in Long Kesh.* Belfast: Sinn Féin

Republican Prisoners, Long Kesh (1975) *Have you No Anger?*
Dublin: Clann na nGaedheal
Republican Prisoners, Long Kesh (1978) *Prison Struggle.*
Belfast: Republican Press Centre
Republican Prisoners, Long Kesh (1988) *Questions of History.*
Dublin: Sinn Féin Education Dept
Robbins, Frank (1977) *Under the Starry Plough.* Dublin: The
Academy Press
Sands, Bobby (1981) *The Diary of Bobby Sands.* Dublin: Sinn
Féin Publicity Department
Sands, Bobby (1981) *The Writings of Bobby Sands.* Dublin:
Sinn Féin POW Department, Dublin
Sands, Bobby (1983) *One Day in My Life.* Dublin: The
Mercier Press
Saunders, Cecilia (1923) *Prison Journal, IE TCD MS 10056*
Seabhac, An (1919) *Jimín.* Baile Átha Cliath: Cómhlucht
Oideachais na hÉireann Teór
Skinnider, Margaret (2016) *Doing My Bit for Ireland.* Dublin:
Republican Publications
The Role of the Language in Ireland's Cultural Revival (1986).
Belfast: Sinn Féin Culture Department
Uí Fhlannagáin, Fionnuala (2008) *Fíníní Mheiriceá agus an
Ghaeilge.* Baile Átha Cliath: Coiscéim
Walsh, Louis J. (1921) *On My Keeping and In Theirs.* Dublin:
Talbot Press
Ward, Margaret (2021) *Unmanageable Revolutionaries.*
Dublin: Arlen House
White, Harry (with Mac Eoin, Uinseann) (1985) *Harry.*
Dublin: Argenta

John Mitchel Library
New South Wales State Library:
The Wild Goose: A Collection of Ocean Waifs. A weekly newspaper
issued on board the convict ship Hougoumont – ed. by J. Flood
and John Boyle O'Reilly. Vol. 1, no. 1-7, (9 Nov. – 21 Dec.),
1867, New South Wales State Library, MLMSS 1542 (Safe 1/409)

Bureau of Military History:
Statement of Dr. Albert Thomas Dryer
https://www.militaryarchives.ie/collections/online-collections/bureau-
of-military-history-1913-1921/reels/bmh/BMH.WS1526.pdf

Statement of Kevin O'Shiel
https://www.militaryarchives.ie/collections/online-collections/bureau-of-military-history-1913-1921/reels/bmh/BMH.WS1770%20Section%206.pdf

Statement of Frank Hardiman:
https://www.militaryarchives.ie/collections/online-collections/bureau-of-military-history-1913-1921/reels/bmh/BMH.WS0406.pdf

Statement of Eamonn O'Dwyer:
https://www.militaryarchives.ie/collections/online-collections/bureau-of-military-history-1913-1921/reels/bmh/BMH.WS1403.pdf

Statement of Ernest Blythe:
https://www.militaryarchives.ie/collections/online-collections/bureau-of-military-history-1913-1921/reels/bmh/BMH.WS0939.pdf

Statement of Frank Thornton:
BMH WS0510

Statement of Art O'Donnell:
https://www.militaryarchives.ie/collections/online-collections/bureau-of-military-history-1913-1921/reels/bmh/BMH.WS1322.pdf

Statement of Liam Roche (de Roiste)
https://www.militaryarchives.ie/collections/online-collections/bureau-of-military-history-1913-1921/reels/bmh/BMH.WS1698%20PART%201.pdf

Statement of Áine Ceant:
https://www.militaryarchives.ie/collections/online-collections/bureau-of-military-history-1913-1921/reels/bmh/BMH.WS0264.pdf

Statement of Laurence Nugent:
https://www.militaryarchives.ie/collections/online-collections/bureau-of-military-history-1913-1921/reels/bmh/BMH.WS0907.pdf

Statement of John Shiel
https://www.militaryarchives.ie/collections/online-collections/bureau-of-military-history-1913-1921/reels/bmh/BMH.WS0928.pdf

National Museum of Ireland:
HE: EW.579 Copy of 'The Rough Tough Truth'. A Journal of
Uncommon Sense, Dundalk Jail, June 1918, Vol. 1 No. 1. Prison
Journal—printed National Museum of Ireland

National Library of Ireland:
https://catalogue.nli.ie/Record/vtls000575135 – John Sarsfield Casey:
Journal of a voyage from Portland to Fremantle on board the
convict ship Hougoumont, ed. Martin Kevin Cusack. National
Library of Ireland original manuscript: MS 49,664/1

https://catalogue.nli.ie/Record/vtls000575127 - Thomas McCarthy
Fennell: 'Life on a Convict Ship' or 'Misery of Penal Exile'

https://catalogue.nli.ie/Record/MS_UR_001692: *The Insect* (1918)
The Insect (1918) Vol 1, No, 1, September 1918 NLI: MS. 24,458
The Insect (1918) manifestos. NLI: MS. 24,458

Joseph S Considine: 'Poems of Prison Camp and Cells', NLI: MS
34,956 A

Saoirse (1921) Issue 1, 9ú Deireadh Fómhair 1921 (P.4) NLI
Holdings: MS 10,913

The Book of Cells (1922) NLI MS 20849

The Trumpeter (1922) Mountjoy: December 3rd 1922 NLI Ms.
21,121 (P.19)

The Catholic Bulletin (1923), Vol. XIII, pp. 604-605, September,
1923. NLI Holdings, Call Number:1H 635

Draft cover of *An Barr Buaidh:*
https://catalogue.nli.ie/Record/MS_UR_077336

Kilmainham Gaol Museum:
An Barr Buaidh (1923) No. 1 'Ag Féachaint Romhainn'. Kilmainham
Prison Museum
C-Weed (1923) May 1923, Foreword. Kilmainham Gaol Museum.

Diary of Hannah Moynihan (1923) KMGLM.2010.0246 (P. 29)

KMGLM.19NW-1D23-28 *The Barbed Wire*, Vol.1, No.1, August, 1921.
KMGLM.2011.0056 Proclamation No. 6453089 B.X.F. (Mountjoy)
KMGLM.2011.0057 *The Trumpeter*, Mountjoy Jail, Vol.1 No.1
KMGLM.2012.0119 *C-Weed*, May 1923, vol. I (Mountjoy)
KMGLM.19NW-1K23-04 *Ná Bac Leis* No 1 Vol 1 Ballykinlar, September 1921
KMGLM.19NW-1D22-15 *Ná Bac Leis* Vol.1 No.2, Ballykinlar, October
KMGLM.2015.0130.01-.05 *Ná Bac Leis*, Vol. 1, No. 3, Ballykinlar, November 1921
KMGLM.20MS-1B42-08 *The NDU Invincible*, 14 May 1923.
KMGLM.20MS-1K56-19 *The Sniper* - Vol 1 No.1 Issued from Mountjoy Jail November 14 1922
KMGLM.20NW-3N22-10 *Poblacht na hEireann/An Phoblacht* Vol 1 No 5 Sporting Edition 24/3/23 (Newbridge)

Newspapers:
Irish Times
Irish News
Derry Journal
Inniú
Lá
Republican News
An Phoblacht
An Phoblacht/Republican News
United Irishman
Nationality

INDEX

ACKNOWLEDGEMENTS

This book probably began more than thirty years ago, when Íte Ní Chionnaith and Seán Mac Mathúna gave me a present one night in Galway of a first edition of *Glimpses of an Irish Felon's Prison Life* by Tom Clarke. Clarke's story told how in an ingenious act of rebellion and subversion against the prison regime, he created his very own newspaper, under the noses of those holding him in prison. That story would come back to me, years later, when I began working on this volume and searching out for other similar prison papers.

In completing the search for these long lost documents I want to acknowledge the help given by Mark McAleese who is a great collector of Irish republican publications and generously gave me access to papers produced in Long Kesh, Magilligan and Armagh Prison. Alasdar Mac Aindreasa gave me access to an incredible source in the unpublished memoir of Liam Ó Muireadhaigh and to Fionnuala Murray for permission to draw from it. Seán Ó Murchadha opened another treasure trove when he gave me copies of extensive minutes from An Cumann Gaelach in Belfast and Derry jails. Ruairí Boyce let me read, and use, his father's unpublished short memoir *Random Thoughts and Reminisces*.

On the website of The John Mitchel Library in New South Wales I found an amazing online set of images of the earliest surviving republican prison paper—from the 1860s—*The Wild Goose*.

Brian Crowley in Kilmainham Gaol brought a long search to conclusion when he let me look through some prison publications from the Civil War-era, while the National Library and Trinity College collections provided a range of diaries and prison papers from the period between the Rising and the end of the Civil War, and from prisons in Ireland and in England and Wales right up to the 1990s. It was a privilege to handle material written by, among others, Traolach Mac Suibhne as far back as 1918, or the jail magazine published by Liam

Mellows and Peadar O'Donnell in 1922. Dr Siobhán Doyle and Clare McNamara from the National Museum of Ireland were very helpful in finding a copy of the Dundalk Jail paper.

I want to thank Anna Bryson for her help in sharing copies of the original prison diary entries of Eamonn Boyce. Séanna Breathnach, Paddy McMenamin, Brendan Curran, and Liam Stone all shared memories and editions of Long Kesh prison newspapers while Laurence Arbuckle, Séamus Keenan and Frankie McCarron all helped with piecing the story of the Magilligan Jail paper together. Marcas Mac Ruairí and Róisín Nic Liam gave me access to papers from Ballykinlar while Kevin Lynch, Paud Mulligan and Mící Ó Cinnsealaigh provided details and copies of the 1990s wing paper in Crumlin Road, plus material from the H-Blocks.

Dermot Connolly, Phil McCullough, Danny Morrison, and Hugh McTigue provided access to some old autograph books and papers from various prisons. Mícheál Breathnach gave me access to his father's prison papers and autograph book from Tintown 1942, including a history lecture, in Irish, from the prison. Aindrias Ó Cathasaigh also helped with information and sources from Fenian times, and on the prisoner/writer, Máirtín Ó Cadhain.

Eamonn Nolan and Ann O'Sullivan and Mick O'Brien provided information on Portlaoise newspapers, while Mark Dawson trawled the files of *An Phoblacht*. Rónan Carson, Séamus Ó Droma, Marrie McNally and Danny Devenny all helped with 1940s and 1950s details from Crumlin Road and the Curragh, while Johnny Haddock—and the Eileen Hickey Museum—all added to my knowledge of Armagh Jail in the 1970s and 1980s, with help also from Síle Darragh, Rose McCartney, Sinéad Walshe and others.

Michael Burns and Joe Keys helped source some of the old images of Derry Jail, as did the Facebook group, Old Photos of Derry People. Tom Hartley facilitated contacts with the Ulster Museum and Peadar Whelan shared some photographs too.

Research carried out by my daughter Eibhlín Nic Cormaic on Feminism, and the Irish language in Armagh Prison in the 1970s-1990s, for her BA degree, and research by my wife Alison Mac Cormaic for her MA in Material Culture examining prison handicrafts, both provided useful information. Dora Uí Challanáin gave me some books which her mother Phil Ní Chuimín wanted me to have, including memoirs by Colm O'Gaora and Earnán de Blaghd, and Paul Butler provided me a copy of *Prison Struggle*. Laurence McKeown added to my recall of

Congress 86, and to the beginning of *Captive Voice/Glór Gafa*. Verena Ní Chuimín helped source difficult to access books. For all these and anyone else who helped I am very grateful.

Thanks to Ruan O'Donnell who read an early draft of the book and offered helpful comments and to Seán Ó Brolcháin and the Irish Republican Felons Association (Felons Club) in West Belfast for their financial support in bringing the book to print.

Particular thanks, however, is reserved for Danny Morrison for his editing, patience and advice and to Seán Mistéil for the layout of the finished work. It goes without saying, of course that any remaining errors are mine.

Finally, go raibh maith agaibh do Alison agus mo pháistí for the encouragement to complete this and other projects.

CUMANN NA MÉIRLEACH
POBLACHTACH ÉIREANNACH

Fill up once more, we'll drink a toast to comrades far away,
No nation on earth can boast of braver hearts than they,
And though they sleep in dungeons deep, or flee outlawed and
  banned
We love them yet, we can't forget, the Felons of our Land.

– The Felons of Our land

Sixty years ago, in 1964, the Irish Republican Felons Association
(Cumann na Méirleach Poblachtach Éireannach) was founded, inspired
by former republican political prisoners who had been in jail in the
1940s and 1950s.

In its humble beginnings it was first housed above Hector's
Hardware Shop on the Falls Road, but it became too small for the
burgeoning membership and so it was moved to Milltown, to a former
Boys Home, an old, moss-covered, dilapidated building, behind
Maguire's Garage on the Falls Road. Access was via a stone bridge over
a small stream. The building was dark and dank, yet it was here that
republicans met and socialised, debated and discussed politics and the
approaching political crisis of August 1969, organised fundraisers,
dances and concerts. All the clubs established at this time and associated
with the Republican Movement were banned by the Stormont
Government, making it an offence under the Special Powers Act to
manage or frequent them.

After the introduction of internment in August 1971 many local
areas opened their own clubs—such as 'the PD [Prisoners Dependents]
Club' (now Andersonstown Social Club), to raise funds for families.

In 1973 the Felons again moved, from the former Boys Home to
537 Falls Road, St Laurence's Hall (its current location), which had no
roof and needed refurbishment. The club became licensed and
subsequently flourished to become a major social hub in West Belfast.

The clubs were subjected to many raids by the British Army and the RUC in attempts to close them down. During scuffles or arrests live rounds and plastic bullets were often discharged, resulting in serious injuries. One of the Felons' bar staff, Liam McKee, was assassinated at his Lisburn home having just returned from his night's work. He had been targeted by a serving member of the British Army's UDR. Two managers of the PD Club, Danny Burke and Jack McCartan in separate incidents, were also shot dead by the British Army at its premises.

Even post-ceasefire, raids on the club and harassment of staff members continued.

The RUC (before its disbandment) raised objections to every renewal of the licence and for over five years pursued a malicious court case against the management which ultimately collapsed.

Today, the Felons Club, or Felons—as it is popularly known—is legendary, not just in Ireland but beyond these shores; is a must-visit spot for tourists; it hosts groups of international students, workshops for former combatants engaged in peace and reconciliation; liaises with organisations representing former prisoners; and expresses its solidarity with other liberation struggles by flying alongside the Tricolour, for example, the flag of beleaguered, but proud, Palestine.

We are honoured to support the publication of *Captive Columns* by former blanket man Eoghan Mac Cormaic; an important work which once again illustrates not just the defiance but also the creativeness, ingenuity, commitment and the unconquerable spirit of those imprisoned felons of our land throughout our long struggle for freedom.

Greenisland Press is an Irish imprint of Elsinor Verlag (Coesfeld, Germany) and is a not-for-profit publishing house. The following titles are generally available but can be purchased from:

An Fhuiseog/The Lark Store, 51/53 Falls Road, Belfast
www.thelarkstore.ie

Sinn Fein Bookshop, 58 Parnell Square, Dublin
www.sinnfeinbookshop.com

An Ceathrú Póilí, An Chulturlann, 216 Falls Road, Belfast
www.anceathrupoili.com/en

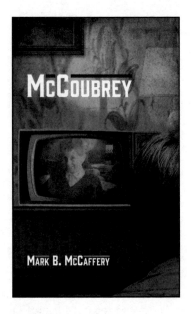

Longlines
JJ Hynes, a veteran IRA activist, has sacrificed everything for the struggle. When an operation goes wrong he finds refuge in Holland before being called back to Ireland to help convince sceptical IRA Volunteers of the merits of the ceasefire and peace process. History, politics, and the possibility of redemption come together in a narrative that reads like a thriller but asks serious and important questions about the interweaving of personal and national trauma.

McCoubrey
A hilarious and enthralling coming-of-age of story set in Portadown, beginning in 1971 as the conflict spreads from Derry and Belfast to engulf small and isolated nationalist communities. Told in the sardonic voice of young Barry-Joe McCaffrey on the cusp of his teens, who reflects on his own life, his family, his troubled neighbourhood—and girls! Barry-Joe rebels against the inconsistencies and double-standards of the world: 'the phonies', as Holden McCaulfield put it.

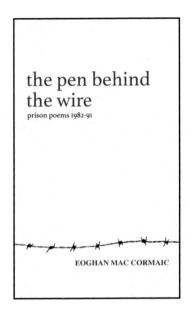

the pen behind
the wire

prison poems 1982-91

EOGHAN MAC CORMAIC

CURIOUS JOURNEY
THE IRA AND CUMANN NA MBAN, 1916 - 1923

Timothy O'Grady & Kenneth Griffith

the pen behind the wire
A selection of poems written by
'Gino' Mac Cormaic when he
was on the blanket protest in the
H-Blocks of Long Kesh (he
served fifteen years in total); and
other poems written after the
prisoners won back their
political status. They allow us to
look with the POWs from their
cell windows out into the wider
world where hopes and dreams
would be realised someday.

Curious Journey
Timothy O'Grady's classic book
first published in 1982 features
interviews with nine republican
veterans who lived into old age
who speak about their struggle
and the tortuous complexities of
a post-Treaty divided Ireland.
Their testimony was recorded at
a time when war again raged in
Ireland in the north-east, a war
hauntingly like the one of their
youth.

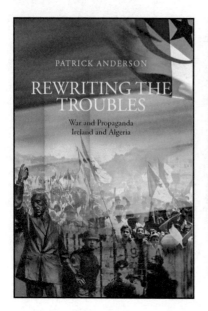

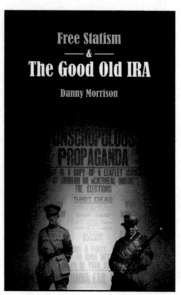

Rewriting The Troubles
Dr Patrick Anderson compares and contrasts Algeria's anti-colonial struggle with the republican campaign to dismantle Britain's colonial legacy. Comparing the French and British armies, the ALN and IRA, loyalists and OAS 'counter-terrorists', Anderson dissects, with devastating effect, the approach of 'constitutional' politicians and the respective media portrayals in an analogy that for critics will be too close for comfort.

Free Statism & The Good Old IRA
The establishment and mainstream media in the South promote a partitionist mind-set – *Free Statism*, argues Morrison—and refuse to prepare for Irish unity. They abandoned northern nationalists to sectarian rule and British repression. They condemned the republican struggle while simultaneously commemorating the IRA campaign during the Tan War as the justifiable deeds of a nation fighting to end British rule in Ireland.